Quick & Easy Way to learn Spanish

Gitika

QUALIS BOOKS

G T BOOK AGENCY

ISBN : 9788187838043

1st Published 2005
Reprinted 2025

Quick & Easy Way to Learn Spanish

Published by
Qualis Books
140, Medha Apartment
Mayur Vihar, Ext. Phase 1,
New Delhi - 110091
E-mail : qualisbooks@yahoo.co.in

Printed in India at
D.K. Fine Art Press (P) Ltd.
Delhi - 110052

Quick & Easy Way to Learn Spanish

This book is intended for any reader who wishes to learn Spanish language & culture in 'Quick and Easy Way' just for personal interest as a student, or is about to travel to this beautiful country. As a result the grammar and the vocabulary have been confined to what might be relevant to such a reader so that the self-learning process does not become a 'put off' on coming across too much of grammar rules.

Abbreviations used in this book-
m-masculine noun
f-feminine noun
mpl-masculine plural
fpl-feminine plural

Inorder to facilitate the pronounciation, each word or sentence in Spanish is followed by its possible equivalent pronounciation in English.

Good luck!

!Buena suerte!

CONTENTS

Part-I
Grammar

Part II
Vocabulary

Part III
Food & Health

Part IV
Travel

Part-I
Chapter 1

GRAMMAR

SPANISH ALPHABETS

Spanish is considered to be one of the most easiest roman languages (German, French, etc.) as far as pronounciation is concerned. The reason is that each alphabet is pronounced very clearly except the alphabet h which is always silent.

Spanish	Pronunciation
A	ah
B	bay
C	say
CH	chay
D	day
E	ay
F	ayfay
G	khay
H	ahchay
I	ee
J	khota
K	kah
L	aylay
LL	ayyay
M	aymay

N	ene
Ñ	eneye
O	oa
P	pay
Q	koo
R	ayray
RR	ayrray
S	aysay
T	tay
U	oo
V	bay
W	ubay doablay
X	aykees
Y	eegryagah
Z	theta

		Spanish	**Pronounciation (in english)**
a	as in class	clase(f)	klaase
b	as in bomb (at the start, after m & n)	bomba(f)	bomba
b	no equivalent in English. bilateral fricative in which lips dont meet.	haber(v)	aber
c	as in keen (before a, o, u or consonant)	claro	klaro
c	as in think (before e, i)	cinco	thinko
ch	as in china	chaqueta	chaketa
d	as in day (at the start, after l, n)	danza	danza
d	as in this (between vowels, after consonants other than l,n)	cada	kada
e	as in they (in open syllable which ends in vowel)	tela	tela
e	as in pet (In closed syllable which ends in consonant)	sangre	sangre
f	as in far	fase	fase

g	no equivalent in English but close to kh (before e,i)	gente	gente
g	as in girl (at the start, after n)	gana	gana
g	as in gay (gue)	guerra	gayrra
	as in guitar (gui)	guiar	guiar
	as in guava (gua)	guardia	guardia
h	always silent	hablar	ablar
i	as in lip	mitad	mitad
j	similar to g above but more aspirated, silent at the end	joya	khoya
k	as in kite	kilo	kilo
l	as in low	levar	levar
ll	as in million	detalle	detalle
m	as in maid	mapa	mapa
n	as in nun (before written v as m)	nada	nada
ñ	as in onion	niña	ninia
o	as in close	otro	otro

	(open syllable ends in vowel)		
o	as in lot (closed syllable ends in consonant)	calor	calor
p	as in push (silent in septiembre)	poner	poner
q	as in pick (always written with u)	querer	kerer
r	as in return but more vibration (like rr at the start,after l, n, s)	rama	rama
rr	no equivalent. more rolled or trilled than r	arriba	arriba
s	as in same (in some cases)	caso	caso
s	as in rise (before b, d, g, l, m, n)	desde	desde
t	as in tale	taza	taza
u	as in root (silent after q, gue, gui except when marked by diaeresis-güiski	luz	luz
v	same as b	verde	verde
w	found in words borrowed from English	whisky	whisky

x	as in ox (between vowels)	taxista	taxista
x	as in big stick	existir	existir
x	as in same (before consonant)	explicar	explicar
y	as in yet	ayuda	ayuda
z	as in thick	zafiro	zafiro
u	as in		
y	as in		

Accent-In Spanish there are clear rules for accentuation of words.

1. Words ending in a consonant except n,s stress the last syllable. e.g. te-a-tro. The syllable 'tro' is stressed.
2. Words ending in a vowel, consonant n, s stress the second last syllable. e.g. u-nos stress on 'u'
3. (i) A dipthong bearing no written accent and composed of a strong (a, e, o) and a weak (i, u) vowel stresses the strong vowel.

   e.g. mien-tras according to rule 2 the stress here is on the syllable 'mien' and according to rule 3 (i) specifically on 'e' since it is a strong vowel.

   (ii) A dipthong bearing no written accent and composed of two weak vowels (ui,iu)stresses the second vowel. e.g. ciu-dad according to rule 1 the stress is on 'ciu' and according to rule 3 (ii) the stress is on 'u'.
4. Words that do not conform to these rules bear a written accent mark over the stressed vowel.

Chapter 2

Articles
Articulos

Indefinite Articles
Articulos Indefinidos

	Singular	Plural
Masculine	un (a, an)	unos
Feminine	una (a, an)	unas

Definite Articles
Articulos Definidos

	Singular	Plural
Masculine	el (the)	los
Feminine	la	las

Chapter 3

Gender & Number
Genero & Numero

Nouns in Spanish are either masculine or feminine. As a general rule:

— words ending with -o, -e are masculine and

— words ending with -a, -ción, -dad are feminine.

But there are few exceptions to the rule.E.g.la mano, el clima.

In order to change numbers a basic rule can be followed.

If the word ends in vowel add -s to make it plural.

E.g. el chico (the boy)

los chicos (the boys)

If the word ends in consonant, stressed í, -z (change -z to -c), add -es to make it plural.

Exception -esquí -esquís. E.g. luz (light) -luces.

Chapter 4

Formation Of Sentences
Formacion De Frases

Generally, in spanish grammar the sentences follow the same order as in english.

She is my sister.
Ella es mi hermana.
Ella es mi ermaana.

Negative Sentences
Just add no before the verb.
I do not play.
(Yo) No juego
(Yo)No khooego

He does not play.
(Él) No juega.
(Él)No khooega.

Note: it is not always necessary to use personal pronouns at the beginning of the sentence because the conjugation of the verb itself denotes the subject unless you wish to emphasize the subject or avoid any confusion about who the subject is.

Note: It is common to use Double Negation with these words- nada (nothing), nadie (nobody), nunca (never). But if these precede the verb no other negation is used after the verb. e.g. No es nunca posible... (It is never ever possible...), Nadie viene... (Nobody comes...)

Interrogative Sentences

Interrogative sentences are as easy to form as negative sentences. Just bring the verb at the beginning of the sentence. The question mark is also put at the beginning of the question but inverted. Another way to form questions is by adding No es verdad or "verdad" to the affirmative sentence.e.g.

The rules are easy. Aren't they?
Las reglas son faciles. ¿verdad? \ ¿no es verdad?
Laas reglas son fathiles ¿verdad?\ ¿no es verdad?

How-
Cómo-
How are you?
¿Cómo está?
¿Kómo está?

How do you spell it?
¿Cómo se escribe?
¿Kómo se eskribe?

Is-
Is there. . .?
¿Hay. . .?
¿Ay?

When-
Cuándo-
Since when?
¿Desde cuándo?
¿Desde kuando?

Till when?
¿Hasta cuándo?
¿Asta kuándo?

What-
Qué-
What is this?
¿Qué es?
¿Ké es?

When is the tren?
¿Cuándo es el tren?
¿Kuándo es l tren?

Where-
Dónde-/Adónde-
Where am I?
¿Dónde estoy?
¿Dónde estoy?

Where are you going?
¿Adónde vas?
¿Adónde vas?

Where are you from?
¿De dónde eres?
¿De dónde eres?

Where is the. . .?
¿Dónde está el /la. . .?
¿Dónde está l /la. . .?

Which-
Cuál-
Which is the room?
¿Cuál es el cuarto?
¿Kuál es l kuarto?

Who-
Quién-
Who is it?
¿Quién es?
¿Kién es?

Whom-
A quién-
Whom did you give?
¿A quién diste?
¿A kién diste?

Whose-
De quién-
Whose is this?
¿De quién es esto?
¿De kién es esto?

Why-
Porqué-
Why are going?
¿Porqué fue?
¿Por ké fue?

Chapter 5

Verbs (Verbos)

Verbs form the core of Spanish language both in terms of importance and magnitude. The reader can also consider it as a warning bell! Though utmost care has been taken to simplify the explanations still the learner is requested to pay here a little more attention...

There are two types of Spanish verbs with regard to conjugation- Regular and Irregular.First let us break the verb in two parts-infinitive and root. e.g.

Verb - cantar(to sing)
Infinitive - ar
Root - habl

There are three types of infinitives-

- ar
- er
- ir

A simple way to form verbs in Present Tense is:

Step 1: Identify the type of infinitve whether -ar, -er or -ir ending and refer to the relevant table below.

Step 2: Separate the infinitive and the root and attach the relevant conjugations to the root taking into consideration the subject of the verb.

	AR	-ER	-IR
I	-o	-o	-o
YOU	-as	-es	es
HE\SHE,etc.	-a	-e	-e

WE	-amos	-emos	-imos
YOU(pl)	-áis	-éis	-ís
THEY\YOU(formal)	-an	-en	-en

Cant-ar (TO SING)

1st person	cant-o (I sing, I am singing)	cant-amos (We sing, We are singing)
2nd person	cant-as (You sing, (You sing,	cant-áis You are singing) You are singing)
3rd person	cant-a (He sings, (They sing,	cant-an He is singing) They are singing)

Note: The hyphen is just to make it easier for you to follow the conjugations.Also note that a single verb form expresses-simple idea-i sing, progressive idea-i am-singing, and can also express the emphatic idea-i do sing.

Com-er (TO EAT)

1st person	com-o (I eat)	com-emos (We eat)
2nd person	com-es (He eats)	com-éis (You (pl.) eat
3rd person	com-e (He eats)	com-en (They eat)

Part-ir

1st person	part-o	part-imos
2nd person	part-es	part-ís
3rd person	part-e	part-en

For IRREGULAR VERBS there is no choice but to memorize them. This is important as well because most of the common and important verbs are irregular. E.g. Ser (be), Estar (be), Hacer (to do), Querer (to want), Gustar (to like), Ver (to see), Ir (to go), poder (be able to), Sentir (to feel), Decir (to speak), etc.

Estar and Ser are two very important verbs in spanish grammar. Although they both signify "be" in english they are used in different contexts in spanish. Generally estar is used for:

1. To denote location e.g.
   Wc arc in Madrid
   Estamos en Madrid
   Estamos en Maadrid
2. With a predicative adjective to express a temporary quality or condition.e.g
   She is very tired today.
   Ella está muy cansada hoy.
   Ella está muy kansada hoy.

On the contrary, ser is used for:

1. With a predicate noun e.g
   -It is my sister's book.
   Es el libro de mi hermana.
   Es l libro de mi ermaana.
2. With predicate adjectives that denote a natural, innate, or permanent quality. e.g.
   -He is a good boy
   Él es un buen chico.
   L es oon booen chiko.

3. In phrases like
   -It is easy to do
   Es fácil hacer
   Es fáthil ather.

   -It is necessary to know
   Es necesario saber.
   Es nethesaario saber.

   -There are 50 of us.
   Somos 50.
   Somos 50.

There are four moods in spanish:

1. Indicative,
2. Conditional(if clause),
3. Imperative(direct commands or request),
4. Subjunctive(negative and indirect commands,to express all kinds of emotions, doubts, give blessings or curses, etc.).

Each mood is expressed in various tenses. For example the indicative mood is expressed in eight tenses but dealing with all of them here may not be possible. Hence the use and conjugation of only four tenses have been taken up.

i. Present-conjugation table for regular verbs given above.
ii. Past Imperfect:
(a) Descriptive sentences\passages in the past.
(b) An action or state going on or continuing in past.
(c) To express a habit, repeated or customary action or state in past time.

	-AR	**-ER + -IR**
-aba	Cant-aba(i was singing)	- ía
-abas	Cant-abas(you were singing)	-ías
-aba	Cant-aba(he\she was singing)	-ía
-ábamos	Cant-ábamos(we were singing)	-íamos
-abais	Cant-abais(you(pl)were singing)	-íais
-aban	Cant-aban(they were singing)	-ían

iii. Preterite:

(a) narrative sentences\passages in the past
(b) an action or state that ended in past

	-AR	**-ER + -IR**
-é	Cant-é(i sang)	-í
-aste	Cant-aste(you sang)	-iste
-ó	Cant-ó(he\she sang)	-ió
-amos	Cant-amos(we sang)	-imos
-asteis	Cant-asteis(you(pl)sang	-isteis
-aron	Cant-aron(they sang)	-ieron

iv. Future:

In the conjugation for this tense the infinitive is not separated from the root of the verb.

	-AR + -ER + -IR
-é	Cantar-é (i will sing)
-ás	Cantar-ás(you will sing)
á	Cantar-á(he\she will sing)
-emos	Cantar-emos(we will sing)
-éis	Cantar-éis(you(pl)will sing)
án	Cantar-án(they will sing)

2. Conditional Mood:

(i) to denote future of past.
(ii) when you want to be courteous
(iii) to denote probability in the past

Here also as in future tense the conjugations are formed alongwith the infinitives intact.

	-AR + -ER + -IR
-ía	Cantar-ía(i would sing)
-ías	Cantar-ías(you would sing)
-ía	Cantar-ía(he would sing)
-íamos	Cantar-íais(we would sing)
-íais	Cantar-íais(you(pl)would sing)
-ían	Cantar-ían(they would sing)

3. Imperative Mood:

(i) informal imperative-subject pronouns Tú and Vosotros are used for singular and plural respectively.

Tú-the imperative conjugation is the same as that of he\she i.e. third person singular in present tense.

E.g. You(to a friend)speak!

¡habla!

Vosotros-replace the r from the infinitives of -ar, -er and -ir with d.

E.g. You (to your cousins) speak!

¡hablad!

(ii) formal imperative-subject pronouns Usted and Ustedes are used for singular and plural respectively.

-AR infinitive-replace the o with e in the first person singular conjugation.

E.g 1st person singular-hablo imperative form-

¡hable!

-ER +IR infinitive-replace the o with a in the first person singular conjugation.E.g 1st person singular-

conjugation-tengo

imperative form-

¡tenga!

4. Subjunctive Mood:

The Subjunctive mood is very commonly used in Spanish.

Just as there were eight tenses in the indicative mood there are, four tenses in the subjunctive mood.

But here only two will be taken up.

(i) Present subjunctive

The regular verb conjugation of this mood:

-AR	**-Er+IR**
-e	-a
-es	-as
-e	-a
-emos	-amos
-éis	-áis
-en	-an

(ii) Past subjunctive

-IF either the principal clause or the dependent clause is in the past tense the subjuctive to be used will be in past.

-IF principal clause is in conditional,the subjuctive will be in past.

-AR	**-ER+IR**
-ara	-iera
-aras	-ieras
-ara	-iera
-áramos	-íeramos
-arais	-ierais
-aran	-ieran

Reflexive Verbs
Verbos Reflexivos

In Spanish, the actions like –to wash,to wake up,to dress up,etc.are more frequently denoted by reflexive verbs than in English by adding suffix 'se' to the verb.E.g.

Lavar (to wash)	Lavarse (to wash oneself)
Despertar (to wake up)	Despertarse (to wake up)
Bañar (to bathe)	Bañarse (to bathe oneself)

The conjugations of the reflexive verbs are the same as that of the general verbs except that the reflexive pronouns precede the verb in indicative case.

Pronouns ***Pronombres***	***Reflexive Pronouns*** ***Pronombres Reflexivo***
YO	ME
TÚ	TE
ÉL,ELLA,USTED	SE
NOSOTROS	NOS
VOSOTROS	OS
ELLOS,ELLAS,USTEDES	SE

They washed themselves.
Ellos se lavaron
Ellos se lavaron

He woke up at eight in the morning,
Èl se despiertó a las ocho de la mañana
L se despiertó a las ocho de la maniana.

She bathed yesterday.
Ella se bañó ayer.
Ella se banió ayer.

Chapter 6

Pronouns
Pronombres

Personal Pronouns
Pronombres Personales

Subject	***Indirect Object***	***Direct Object***
YO-i	ME-to me	ME-me
Tú-you (informal)	TE-to you	TE-you
Él-he	LE-to him	LE-him
ELLA-she	LE-to her	LA-her
	LE-to it	LO-it
USTED(m)-you (formal)	LE-to you (formal)	LE-you
USTED(f)-you (formal)	LE-to you (formal)	LA-you
NOSOTROS (m) -we	NOS-to us	NOS-us
NOSOTROS (f) -we	NOS-to us	NOS-us
VOSOTROS-you (plural informal)	OS-to you	OS-you
ELLOS-they	LES-to them	LOS-them
ELLAS (f) -they	LES-to them	LAS-them
USTEDES (m) -you (plural formal)	LES-to you	LOS-you
USTEDES (f) -you (plural formal)	LES-to you	LAS-you

RULE 1: Generally,all personal pronoun objects are placed before the verb.E.g.

I will tell you all about it.
Te lo diré todo
Te lo diré todo.

RULE 2: When indirect and direct object pronouns are to be used together,place the indirect object pronoun before the direct one.E.g.

She sells it to us.
Ella nos lo/la vende.
Ella nos lo/la vende.

Lo/la will depend whether the direct object pronoun "it"stands for a masculine noun or a feminine one.

RULE 3: If the verb is infinitive,and both direct and indirect object pronouns are to be used then they both are placed after the verb.E.g.

He is going to tell it to me.
Él va a decírmelo.
Él va a detheermelo

RULE 4: If third person indirect object pronoun is followed by third person direct object pronoun,then indirect object pronoun becomes se.E.g.

We give it to her.
Se lo/la damos a ella
Se lo/la damos a ella

("a ella" is added for clarification that the indirect object pronoun is feminine(her).Similarly,

We give it to him
Se lo/la damos a él.
Se lo/la damos a él

Personal pronouns
(used as subjects of verbs)

	Singular	**Plural**
1st person	I- YO	We-nosotros(m) -nosotras(f)
2nd person	You-Tú (informal)	Vosotros(m) Vosotras(f)
3rd person	He-Él She-Ella You(formal)- Usted	They-Ellos(m) They-Ellas(f) You(formal)-Ust- edes

Note: Tú and vosotros are used in addressing relatives, friends, and children under 12-14 years of age. Usted is commonly abbreviated as Vd. and Ustedes as Vds.

Possessive Pronouns

Possessive Adjectives **Adjetivos Posesivos**		**Possessive Pronouns** **Pronombres Posesivos**
	Singular	**Plural**
Mi	El mío (m), La mía (f)	Los míos (mpl), Las mías (fpl)
Tu	El tuyo (m), La tuya (f)	Los tuyos (mpl), Las tuyas (fpl)
Su	El suyo (m), La suya (f)	Los suyos (mpl), Las suyas (fpl)
Nuestro	El nuestro (m)	Los nuestros (mpl)
Nuestra	La nuestra (f)	Las nuestras (fpl)
Vuestro	El vuestro (m)	Los vuestros (mpl)
Vuestra	La vuestra (f)	Las vuestras (fpl)

Remember that the possessive pronouns must agree with their antecedents in gender and number.

Demonstrative Pronouns
(Pronombres Demonstrativos)

	Singular	**Plural**
This,These	Éste,Ésta	Éstos,Éstas
That,Those	Ése,Ésa	Ésos,Ésas
That,Those	Aquél,Aquélla	Aquéllos,Aquéllas

Note : The demonstrative pronouns have written accents to distinguish them from the demonstrative adjectives.

Éste denotes something near the speaker.
Ése denotes something near the person addressed.
Aquél denotes something remote from both.

Note: Éste –Which also means 'the latter' is mentioned before Aquél- 'the former' in Spanish.

Chapter 7

Active And Passive Voice
Voz Activa Y Pasiva

In Spanish grammar,active voice is the same as in English.The passive voice is not much used.

(i) The passive idea be changed into an active one

The work is done.
Hacemos el trabajo (We do the work)
Athemos l trabakho.

(ii) The passive idea is not changed. The sentence begins with "se" or "no se" followed by the verb in third person singular. The tense is present if the helping verb is in present tense.

The work is done
Se hace el trabajo
Se athe l trabakho

(iii) To avoid using "se"or "no se",the verb in third person plural is used to express the same passive idea.

The work is done
Hacen el trabajo
Athen l trabakho

More examples:

Spanish is spoken here.

(i) Se habla español aquí.
Se abla espaniol akí

(iii) Hablan español aquí
Ablan espaniol akí
Hindi is not spoken here.

(i) No se habla hindi aquí.
No se abla indi akí

(iii) No hablan hindi aquí.
No ablan indi akí

This pen was made here.
Esta pluma fue hecha aquí
Esta pluma fue echa akí.

In this example the auxiliary "ser" and the perfect participle of hacer(hecho/hecha)is used.Remember that the perfect participle just like the adjective must agree with the subject in gender and number.

These pens were made here.
Estas plumas fueron hechas aquí.
Estas plumas fueron echas akí

When a passive state instead of a passive act has to be described,the auxiliary Spanish verb "estar" is used.E.g.

His bag is open.
Su bolso está abierto.
Su bolso está abierto

Chapter 8

Adjectives & Adverbs
Adjetivos & Adverbios

Possessive Adjectives
Adjetivos Posesivos

Singular	**Plural**	**Usage**
mi	mis	my
tu	tus	your(to a friend)
nuestro(m)	nuestros(m)	our
nuestra(f)	nuestras(f)	
vuestro(m)	vuestros(m)	your(to friends)
vuestra(f)	vuestras(f)	
su	sus	his, her, its, their, your(formal)

Remember that the possessive adjective must agree in gender and number with the noun it modifies.

Note:

	-my sister	-my sisters
	mi hermana	mis hermanas
	mi ermaana	mis ermaanas
	-our sister	-our sisters
	nuestra hermana	nuestras hermanas
	nooestra ermaana	nooestra ermaanas
	-our brother	-our brothers
	nuestro hermano	nuestros hermanos
	nooestro ermaano	nooestro ermaanos

A\The dirty room.
Un\El cuarto sucio.
Un\l kuaarto suthio.

The dirty rooms.
Los cuartos sucios.
Los kuaartos suthios.

A\The dirty cloth.
Una\La ropa sucia.
Una\La ropa suthia.

The dirty clothes.
Las ropas sucias.
Las ropas suthias.

In English, adverbs are often formed by adding *–ly* to the adjective:sure,sure*ly*; quiet,quiet*ly*. In Spanish,adverbs are generally formed in a similar way,by adding *–mente* to the feminine singular of the adjective.

Adjective		*Adverb*	
Masculine singular	**Fem.sing**		
Claro(Clear)	Clara	Clara*mente* (Clearly)	Klaramente
Cuidadoso(Careful)	Cuidadosa	Cuidadosa*mente* (Carefully)	Kuidadosamente
Sincero(Sincere)	Sincera	Sincera*mente* (Sincerely)	Sintheramente
Fácil(Easy)	Fácil	Fácil*mente* (Easily)	Fáthilmente
Amable (Pleasant person)	Amable	Amable*mente* (Pleasantly)	Amablemente

Agradable (Pleasant weather)	Agradable	Agradable*mente* (Pleasantly)	Agradablemente
Cortés(Courteous)	Cortés	Cortés*mente* (Courteously)	Cortésmente
Alegre(Happy)	Alegre	Alegre*mente* (Happily)	Alegremente
Rico(rich)	Rica	Rica*mente* (Richly)	Rikamente
Feliz(Happy)	Feliz	Feliz*mente* (Happily)	Felithmente
Afortunado (Fortunate)	Fortunada	Fortunada*mente* (Fortunately)	Fortunadamente
Principal(Main)	Principal	Principalmente (Mainly)	Printhipaalmente

Some common adverbs that do not end in *–mente*:

Bien	Well	Rita sings very well. Rita canta muy bien. Rita kanta muy bien
Mal	Badly	Everything turned out badly. Todo salió mal. Todo salió maal
Demasiado	Too	It's too late Es demasiado tarde Es demaasiaado tarde
Poco	Little, Small	A little more,please Um poco más,por favor Um poko más por favor

Tanto	So much, As much	He spends as much as I do. Él gasta tanto como yo L gasta taanto komo yo
Siempre	Always	Why is he always sad? Por qué é siempre triste? Por ké é siempre
En seguida	Immediately	The train left immediately. El tren salió en seguida L tren salió en seguida
Aquí	Here	This book is here. Este libro está aquí. Este libro está akí
Allá	Over there	That book is over there. Aquele libro está allá Akele libro está allá
Allí	There	That book is there. Esse libro está aquí. Esse libro está akí

Demonstrative Adjectives
Adjetivos Demonstrativos

	Singular	**Plural**
This,These	Este,Esta	Estos,Estas
That,Those	Ese,Esa	Esos,Esas
That,Those	Aquel,Aquella	Aquellos,Aquellas

Also remember to repeat the demonstrative adjective before each word that it modifies.E.g.

This is his son and that is my son..
Este es su hijo y ese es mi hijo
Este es su ikho e ese es mi ikho

Comparison Of Adjective
Comparacion De Adjetivos

Unlike in English where comparisons can by(i) either adding *–er* or *–est* to some adjectives and adverbs or by (ii)placing "more" or "less";"most" or "least" before these and other adjectives and adverbs; in Spanish,the comparative and superlative degrees are alike and both are formed by putting "*más*"(more),*el más*(most) or "*menos*"(less),*el menos*(least)before the adjective or adverb.In adjectives the definite article in *el más* and *el menos* must agree in gender and number with the accompanying noun.

.E.g.The richest man
El hombre más rico
L ombre más riko

The richest women
Las mujeres más ricas
Las mukheres más rikas

Positive	**Comparative**	**Superlative**
Positivo	**Comparativo**	**Superlativo**
Fuerte(Strong)	*Mais* fuerte(Stronger)	*El mais* fuerte(Strongest)
Rico(Rich)	*Mais* rico(Richer)	*El mais* rico(Richest)

E.g. Radha is rich but Mona is richer.Rita is the richest.
Radha es rica pero Mona es *más* rica.Rita es *la más* rica
Radha es rika pero Mona es más rika.Rita es la más rika.

My trip was very interesting. Meena's trip was less interesting.
Sunny's trip was the least interesting.
A mía viaje fui muy interesante. El viaje de Meena fui *menos* interesante.El viaje de Sunny fui *el menos* interesante.

The word *than* used in comparisons in English is generally translated as *que* or *de que* in Spanish.E.g.

I learnt much more *than* you.
Yo aprendí mucho más *que* tú
Yo aprendí mucho más ke tú

I ate less *than* you.
Comí menos que tú
Comí menos ke tú

As much . . .as in English is translated as *tan(tanto). . .como*

She travels as much as i do.
Ella viaja tanto como yo.
Ella viakha tanto komo yo.

He works as happily as i do.
Él trabaja tan alegremènte como yo.
L trabakha tan alegremente komo yo.

The more/less. . .the more/less in English is expressed as *cuanto más/menos. . .tanto más/menos* .*Tanto* can be omitted.E.g.

The more i travel here,the more i like this place.
Cuanto más viajo,(tanto)más me gusta este lugar.
Kuanto más viakho,(tanto)más me goosta este loogar.

The less i drink tea, the more tired I feel
Cuanto menos tomo el té, (tanto)más me siento cansado/a
Kuanto menos tomo l té, (tanto) más me siento kansado/a

Irregular Comparative Forms (Formas Irregulares Comparativas)

Some very common adjectives and adverbs have irregular forms of comparison.

Adjective	**Comparative**	**Superlative**	
ADJETIVO	COMPARATIVO	SUPERLATIVO	
Bueno(Good)	Mejor(Better)	El mejor(Best)	L mekhor
Malo(Bad)	Peor(Worse)	El peor(Worst)	L peor
Grande(Big)	Mayor(Bigger)	El mayor(Biggest)	L mayor

NOTE: Mayor, referring to persons, usually means older, oldest.

Adverb	**Comparative**	**Superlative**
Bien(Well)	Mejor(Better)	El mejor(Best)
Mal(Badly)	Peor(Worse)	El peor(Worst)
Muy(Very)	Más(More)	El más(Most)
Poco(Little)	Menos(Less)	El menos(Least)

The Absolute Superlative (El Superlativo Absoluto)

Spanish frequently uses the adjective or adverb form that ends in *–ísimo*.

When the basic adjective ends in an unstressed vowel, drop the vowel and add *–ísimo*.E.g.

Alto (High)	Alto	Altísimo (very high)

But not all follow the same rule.E.g.

Rico (Rich)	Riquísimo (Very rich)
Largo (Long)	Larguísimo (Very long)
Chico (small)	Chiquito (Very small)

When the adverb ends in *–mente*,it is replaced by *–ísimo* E.g.

Alegremente (Happily)	Alegr*ísimo*(Very happy)
Mucho(Much)	Much*ísimo*(Very much)

Even diminutive forms are also used to denote size or express affection, love.

Word **Palabra**	**Pronounciation** **Pronunciacion**	**Diminutive** **Diminutivo**	**Pronounciation** **Pronunciacion**
Pequeño (Small)	Pekenio	Pequenito (Very small)	Pekenito
Chico (Boy)	Chiko	Chiquito	Chikito
Chica (Girl)	Chika	Chiquita	Chikita
Hijo (Son)	Ikho	Hijito	Ikhito
Años (Age, Years)	Anios	Añitos	Anietos
Coche (Car)	Koche	Cochecito	Kochethito
Casa(House)	Kasa	Casita	Kasita

It is common custom to use diminutive form of proper names to express affection or familiarity with the person.

Name **Nombre**		**Diminutive** **Diminutivo**	
Juan(m)	Khuan	Juanito	Khuanito
Juana(f)	Khuana	Juanita	Khuanita

Chapter 9

Model Letters
Cartas Modelas

I. Correspondencia Comercial

New delhi

Dierctor
Aceituna Popular
Puerta del Sol,6
Madrid

16 March 2005

Dear Sir,
I would like to seek more information about the products of your company and whether you have any plans to open franchise(s)in India in the near future.
We look forward to hearing from you.

Yours faithfully
Ashok Saxena

Nova Delhi,16 de marzode2005

Director
Aceituna Popular
Puerta del sol,6
Madrid

Estimado Señor,
Me dijo usted para solicitar mayor informción sobre los productos de su compañía y si hace proyectos en fecha próxima para abrir franquicia(s)en la India.

Sin otro particular,quedamos a la espera de sus noticias.

Le saluda atentamente,
Ashok Saxena

Personal Correspondence: Correspondencia Personal

New Delhi
16th March 2005

Dear Meera,

It was lovely to hear from you after such a long time.Please forgive me for not having written before.I am very busy here.Please remember me to your sister.I am also inviting you to spend a few weeks here.The weather is lovely here!The very best of luck for your exam.

Hoping to hear from you.
Love,
Mona.

Nova Deli,
16 de marzo, 2005

Querida Meera,

Me alegró mucho recibir noticias tuyas después de tanto tiempo.Perdona que no te haya escrito antes.Estoy muy ocupada aquí.Dele mis recuerdos a tu hermana.Te invito a pasar unas semanas aquí.Hace buen tiempo aquí!Te deseo toda la suerte del mundo en el examen.

Quedo a la espera de sus noticias.
Un abrazo de
Mona.

Chapter 10

Filling Form
Llenar Hoja

Mr.	Señor
Sir	Don
Miss	Señorita
Mrs.	Señora
Madam	Doña
Nombre	name
Apellido(s)	surname(s)
Domicilio	address(residence)
Avenida	avenue
Callejón	lane
Calle	street
Nacionalidad	nationality
Fecha da nacimiento	date of birth
Lugar de nacimiento	place of birth
Profesión	profession
Núm.de Pasaporte	passport no.
Exp.en	issued at
Fecha	date
Grupo sanguíneo	blood group
Firma	signature

Chapter 11

Proverbs
Proverbios

(A)

A bird in hand is worth two in the bush.
Más vale pájaro en mano que ciento volando.
Más vale pákharo en maano ke thiento volaando.

A man is known by the company he keeps.
Dime con quién andas y diré quién eres.
Dime kon kién aandaas y diré kién eres.

A rolling stone gathers no moss.
Piedra movediza nunca moho la cobija.
Piedra moveditha noonka moo la kobikha.

A stich in time saves nine
Una puntada a tiempo ahorra ciento.
Una poontaada tiempo aorra thiento/
Quien acude a la gotera acude a la casa.
Kien akoode a la gotera akoode a la kasa.

(B)

Beggars can't be choosers
A quien dan no escoge./ A kien daan no eskokhe.
Los pobres no escogen./ Los pobres no eskokhen.

Better late than never.
Más vale tarde que nunca.
Más vale taarde ke noonka.

Birds of a feather flock together.
Dios los cría y ellos se juntan.
Dios los kría y ellos se khuntaan.

By hook or by crook.
Como sea,por las buenas o por las malas.
Komo sea,por las booenaas o por las maalas.

(E)

Easy come easy go.
Así se viene y así se va.
Así se viene y así se va.

Every cloud has a silver lining.
No hay mal que por bien no venga.
No hay maal ke por bien no venga.

(F)

Familiarity breeds comtempt.
Lo conocido no se estima.
Lo konothido no se estima.

(I)

It's no good crying over spilt milk.
A lo hecho pecho,agua pasada no mueve molino.
Alo echo pecho,agooa pasada no mooeve molino.

It's blood is thicker than water.
La sangre es más espesa que el océano
La saangre es más espesa ke l océaano.

(L)

Let sleeping dogs lie.
Vale más no meneallo.
Vale más nomeneallo.

Life isn't exactly a bed of roses.
La vida no es ningún lecho de rosas.
La vida no es ningún lecho de rosaas.

Life begins at 40.
La vida comienza a los 40.
La vida komientha a los 40.

(M)

Man proposes,God disposes.
El hombre propone y Dios dispone.
L ombre propone y Dios dispone.

Might is right.
Es la ley del más fuerte.
Es la ley del más fooerte.

(R)

Rome was not built in a day.
No se ganó Zamora en una hora.
No se ganó Thamora en oona ora.

(S)

Silence is golden.
El silencio es de oro.
L silenthio es de oro.

(T)

The early bird catches the worm.
Al que madruga Dios le ayuda.
Al ke maadrugaa Dios le ayuda.

The end justifies the means.
El fin justifica los medios.
L fin khustifika los medios.

There's many a slip 'twixt cup and lip.
De la mano a la boca desaparece la sopa.
De la maano a la boka desaparethe la sopa.

They are birds of a feather.
Son lobos de una camada.
Son lobos de una kaamada.

Those that live by the sword die by the sword.
El que a hierro mata a hierro muere.
L ke a ierro maata a ierro mooere.

To be between the devil and the deep blue sea.
Estar entre la espada y la pared.
Estar entre la espaada y la pared.

To beat about the bush
Ir con rodeos
Ir kon rodeos.

To build castles in the air.
Construir castillos en el aire.
Konstruir kastillos en l aire.

To call a spade a spade.
Llamar al pan y al vino vino.
Llamaar al paan y al vino vino.

To spare the rod and spoil the child.
Quien bien te quiere te hará llorar.
Kien bien te kiere te ará llorar.

To strike while the iron is hot.
A hierro candente batir de repente.
A ierro kandente baatir de repente.

To kill two birds with one stone.
Matar dos pájaros de un tiro.
Matar dos pákharos de un tiro.

To make hay while the sun shines.
Hacer su agosto.
Ather su aagosto.

To reap what one has sown.
Cosechar lo que uno ha sembrado.
Kosechar lo ke uno a sembrado.

To want to have one's cake and eat it.
Querer nadar y guardar la ropa.
Querer naadar y gooardar la ropa.

Two's company but three's a crowd.
Con dos basta y sobra uno.
Kon dos baasta y sobra oono

(W)

When in Rome do as the Romans do.
Allí donde fueres haz lo que vieres.
Allí donde fooeres hath lo ke vieres.

Where there's a will there's a way.
Querer es poder .
Kerer es poder.

Part-II
Chapter 1

Parts Of The Body
Las Partes Del Cuerpo

English	Spanish	Pronunciation
Abdomen	abdomen(m)	abdomen
Ankle	tobillo(m)	tobilyo
Appendix	apéndice	apéndithe
Arm	brazo(m)	bratho
Armpit	sobaco(m)	sobakσ
Back	espalda(f)	espaalda
Beard	barba(f)	barba
Belly	vientre(m)	vientre
Bladder	vejiga(f)	vekhiga
Blood	sangre(f)	saangre
Body	cuerpo(m)	kuerpo
Bone	hueso(m)	ooeso
Bosom	seno(m)	seno
Brain	cerebro(m)	cerebro
Breast	pecho(m)	pecho
Cheek	mejilla(f)	mekhilla
Chest	pecho(m)	pecho
Chin	barba(f)	barba
Collarbone	clavícula(f)	klavíkula
Diaphragm	diafragma(m)	diafragma
Diastole	diástole(f)	diástole
Ear	oreja(f)	orekha

Elbow	codo(m)	kodo
Eye	ojo(m)	okho
Eyeball	globo(m) de ojo	globo de okho
Eyebrow	ceja(f)	cekha
Eyelash	pestaña(f)	pestania
Eyelid	párpado(m)	páarpaado
Face	cara(f)	kara
Finger	dedo(m)	dedo
Fist	puño(m)	punio
Flesh	carne(f)	karne
Foot	pie(m)	pie
Forehead	frente(f)	frente
Gall-bladder	vesícular(f)biliar	vesíkulaar biliaar
Gum	encía(f)	enthíaa
Hair	pelo(m)	pelo
Hand	mano(f)	maano
Head	cabeza(f)	kabetha
Heart	corazón(m)	koraathón
Heel	talón(m)	taalón
Hip	cadera(f)	kadera
Intestine	intestino(m)	intestino
Joint	articulación(f)	artikulathión
Knee	rodilla(f)	rodilla
Kidney	riñón(f)	rinión
Large intestine	intestino(m)grueso	intestino grooeso
Leg	pierna(f)	pierna
Lip	labio(m)	laabio
Liver	hígado(m)	ígaado
Lung	pulmón(m)	pulmón
Moustache	bigote(m)	beegote
Mouth	boca(f)	boka

Muscle	músculo(m)	múskulo
Nail	uña(f)	unia
Neck	cuello(m)	kuello
Nerve	nervio(m)	nervio
Nose	nariz(f)	naarith
Palm	palma(f)	paalma
Penis	pene(m)	pene
Rib	costilla(f)	kostilla
Ribcage	tórax	tóraax
Shoulder	hombro(m)	ombro
Sinus	seno(m)	seno
Skin	piel(f)	piel
Skull	cráneo(m)	kráaneo
Small intestine	intestino(m)delgado	intestino delgaado
Sole	planta(f)	planta
Spine	espinazo(m)	espinatho
Stomach	estómago(m)	estómaago
Systole	sístole(f)	sístole
Temple	sien(f)	sien
Thigh	muslo(m)	muslo
Throat	garganta(f)	gaargaanta
Thumb	pulgar(m)	pulgaar
Toe	dedo(m)del pie	dedo del pie
Tongue	lengua(f)	lengooa
Tooth	diente(M)	diente
Vein	vena(f)	vena
Vertebra	vértebra(f)	vértebra
Waist	cintura(F)	thintura
Wrist	muñeca(F)	munieka

Chapter 2

Climate
Clima

1. Hacer is a common verb used while describing weather wherever 'be+adjective' is used in english.

be cold-hacer frío
It will be (very) cold tomorrow.
Hará (mucho) frío mañana.
Ará (mucho) frío maniana.

be hot-hacer calor
It was (very) hot last night.
Hizo (mucho) calor anoche.
Itho (mucho) kalor anoche.

It was a very hot day.
Fue un día de mucho calor.
Fue un día de moocho kalor.

be bad (good) weather-hacer mal (buen) tiempo
The weather is going to be bad.
Va a hacer mal tiempo.
Va a ather maal tiempo.

The weather is very fine.
Hace muy buen tiempo.
Athe muy buen tiempo.

What will the weather be like tomorrow?
¿Qué tiempo hará mañana?
¿Ké tiempo ará maniana?

be sunshine-hacer sol
The sun is not shining.
No hace sol
No athe soul.

be cool-hacer fresco
It is cool today
Hace fresco hoy.
Athe fresco oy.

It is pleasantly warm.
Hace un calor agradable.
Athe un kalor agradaable.

From sunrise to sunset
De sol a sol.
De soul a soul.

In the sunshine
Al sol
Al soul

What is the temperature?
¿Qué es la temperatura?
¿Ké es la temperatoora?

The temperature is 5 degrees below freezing.
La temperatura es 5 grados bajo cero.
La temperatura es 5 graados bakho thero.

What is the weather forecast?
¿Qué es el pronóstico del tiempo?
¿Ké es l pronóstiko del tiempo?

What are the weather conditions of Madrid?
¿Qué es el estado del tiempo de Madrid?
¿Ké es l estaado del tiempo de Madrid?

It is windy today.
Hoy hace viento.
Oy athe viento.

Chapter 3

Animals
Animales

English	Spanish	Pronunciation
Animal	animal(m)	aanimaal
Bull	toro(m)	toro
Bullock	toro(m) castrado	toro kastraado
Buffalo	búfalo(m)	búufaalo
Bitch	perra(f)	perra
Calf	ternero(m), ternera(f)	ternero, ternera
Cat	gato(m)	gaato
Chamelion	camaleón(m)	kamaaleón
Camel	camello(m)	kamello
Cow	vaca(f)	vaaka
Dangerous	peligroso(m)	peligroso
Dangerous	peligrosa(f)	peligrosa
Deer	ciervo(m)	thiervo
Dog	perro(m)	perro
Donkey	burro(m), burra(f)	burro, la burra
Elephant	elefante(m), elefanta(f)	elefante, elefanta
Endangered	peligro de extinción	peligro de-extinthión
Fox	zorra(F)	thorra
Goat (m)	macho cabrío(m)	macho kabrío
Goat (f)	cabra(f)	kabra
Hare	liebre(f)	liebre
Heifer	novilla(f)	novilla
Horse	caballo(m)	kaballo
Hound	podenco(m)	podenko

Indian elephant	elefante(m)asiático	elefante asiátiko
Jackal	chacal(m)	chakaal
Lamb	cordero(M) cordera(f)	kordero, kordera
Leopard	leopardo(m)	leopaardo
Lion	león(m) leona(f)	león,leonaa
Mare	yegua(f)	yegooaa
Mongoose	mangosta(f)	maangostaa
Monkey	mono(M), mona(f)	mono, mona
Mouse	ratón(m)	raatón
Mule	mulo(m), mula(f)	moolo, moola
Pig	cerdo(m)	therdo
Protected	protegido(m)	protekhido
Protected	protegida(f)	protekhida
Pup	cachorro(m)	kachorro
	cachorra(f)	kachorra
Python	pitón(m)	pitón
Ram	carnero(m)	karnero
Rhinoceros	rinoceronte(m)	rinotheronte
Sheep	oveja(f)	ovekha
Skunk	mofeta(f)	mofeta
Snake	serpiente(f)	serpiente
Squirrel	ardilla(f)	ardilla
Stag	ciervo(m)	thiervo
Swine	puerco(m)	pooerko
Tiger	tigre(m)	tigre
Tom	gato(m)	gaato
Wolf	lobo(m), loba(f)	lobo, loba
Crab	cangrejo(m)	kangrekho
Crocodile	cocodrilo(m)	kokodrilo
Fish	pez(m)	peth
Leech	sanguijuela(f)	sangeekhuelaa
Tortoise	tortuga(f)	tortuga

Chapter 4

Birds
Aves

English	Spanish	Pronunciation
Bat	murciélago(m)	murthiélaago
Bird	pájaro(m)ave(f)	pákharo,ave
Cock	gallo(m)	gallo
Crane	grulla(f)	grulla
Crow	cuervo(m)	kuervo
Cuckoo(m)	cuco(m)	kuko
Dove	paloma(f)	paalomaa
Duck	pato(m)	paato
Hen	gallina(f)	gaallina
Kite	milano(M) real	milaano reaal
Nightingale	ruiseñor(m)	ruisenior
Owl	lechuza(f)	lechutha
Parrot	loro(m)	loro
Partridge	perdiz(f)	perdith
Peacock	pavo(m) real	paavo reaal
Pigeon	paloma(f)	paalomaa
Sparrow	gorrión(m)	gorrión
Swan	cisne(m)	thisne
Vulture	buitre(m)	buitre

Chapter 5

Insects
Insectos

English	Spanish	Pronunciation
Ant	hormiga(f)	ormiga
Bee	abeja(f)	aabekha
Bug	chinche(f)	chinche
Butterfly	mariposa(f)	maariposaa
Fly	mosca(f)	moska
Frog	rana(f)	rana
Germ	germ(m)	kherm
Glowworm	luciérnaga(f)	luthiérnaaga
Insect	insecto(M)	insekto
Lizard	lagarto(m)	laagaarto
Locust	langosta(f)	laangostaa
Mosquito	mosquito(m)	moskito
Scorpion	escorpión(m)	eskorpión
Spider	araña(f)	arania
Snail	caracol(m)	karakol
Wasp	avispa(f)	aavispa

Chapter 6

Plants & Flowers
Plantas & Flores

English	Spanish	Pronunciation
Acacia	acacia(f)	akathia
Balsamo	bálsamo(m)	báalsaamo
Chrysanthemum	crisantemo(m)	krisaantemo
Daisy	maya(f)	maya
Indian hemp	cáñamo(m)índico	kániamo índiko
Jasmine	jazmín(m)	khathmín
Lilac	lila(f)	lila
Lily	lirio(m)	leereeo
Lotus	loto(m)	loto
Magnolia	magnolia(f)	magnoleea
Marigold	caléndula(f)	kaléndula
Mushroom	seta(f)	seta
Myrtle	mirto(m)	meerto
Narcissus	narciso(m)	narthiso
Rose	rosa(f)	rosa

Chapter 7

House & House Hold Articles
Casa & Articulos Domesticos

English	Spanish	Pronunciation
Abattoir	matadero(m)	matadero
Ante-chamber	antecámara	antekámara
Apartment house	casa(f)de pisos	kasa de pisos
Arch	arco(m)	arko
Armchair	sillón(m)	sillón
Attic	ático(m)	áatiko
Air freshener	ambientador(m)	ambientador
Ash tray	cenicero(m)	thenithero
Balcony	balcón(m)	balkón
Barrack	caserón(m)	kaserón
Beam	viga(f)	viga
Basket	cesta(f)	thesta
Bathmat	estera(f)de baño	estera de banio
Bathroom	cuarto(m)de baño	kuarto de banio
Bath-salts	sales(fpl)de baño	sales de banio
Bath-sheet	toalla(f)de baño	toalla de banio
Bath-towel	toalla(f)de baño	toalla de banio
Bathtub	bañera(f)	baniera
Battlements	almenas(fpl)	aalmenaas
Bed	cama(f)	kama
Bedroom	alcoba(f)	alkoba
Bedsheet	sobrecama(f)	sobrekama
Bedspread	sobrecama(f)	sobrekama
Bench	banco(m)	banko

Blanket	manta(f)	manta
Bolster	travesero(m)	travesero
Bottle	botella(f)	botella
Bottle opener	abrebotellas(m)	abrebotellas
Bowl	bol(m)	bol
Box	caja(f)	kakha
Bracket	ménsula(f)	ménsoola
Brick	ladrillo(m)	ladrillo
Broom	escoba(f)	eskoba
Brush	cepillo(m)	thepillo
Bucket	cubo(m)	kubo
Building	edificio(m)	edifithio
Bulb	bombilla(f)	bombilla
Bungalow	bungalow(m)	boongalow
Cabinet	armario(m)	armaario
Candle	vela(f)	vela
Candlestick	candelero(m)	kaandelero
Canister	lata(f)	lata
Carpet	alfombra(f)	aalfombra
Can opener	abrelatas(m)	abrelatas
Carpet tile	loseta(f)	loseta
Casket	cajita(f)	kakhita
Ceiling	techo(m)	techo
Censer	incensario(m)	inthensaario
Chair	silla(f)	silla
Chandelier	araña(f) de luces	arania de luthes
Chimney	chimenea(f)	chimenea
Chopping board	tabla(f)para cortar	tabla para kortar
Churner	lechera(f)	lechera
Cigarette-Lighter	mechero(m)	mechero

Cloister	claustro(m)	klaustro
Closet	lavabo(m)	lavaabo
Closet(for clothes)	ropero(m)	ropero
Clothes-basket	canasta(f)de la-ropa sucia	kanasta de la-ropa soothia
Clothes-brush	cepillo(m)de la ropa	thepillo de la ropa
Clothes-drier	secadora(f)	sekadora
Clothes-hanger	percha(f)	percha
Clothes-line	cuerda(f)de tendedero	kuerda de-tendedero
Clothes-moth	polilla(f)	polilla
Clothespeg	pinza(f)	pintha
Clothespole	palo(m)de tendedero	paalo de-tendedero
Clothes-rack	tendedero(m)	tendedero
Compact disk	disco(m)compacto	disko kompakto
Computer	ordenador(m)	ordenador
Corkscrew	sacacorchos(m)	sakakorchos
Corridor	pasillo(m)	pasillo
Cottage	casita(f)de campo	kasita de kampo
Couch	canapé(m)	kanapé
Courtyard	patio(m)	patio
Cup	taza(f)	tatha
Cupboard(on wall)	alacena(f)	alathena
Curtain	cortina(f)	kortina
Cushion	cojín(m)	kokhín
Cutlery	cubiertos(mpl)	kubiertos
Dais	estrado(m)	estraado
Dining-hall	comedor(m)	komedor
Dining-room	comedor(m)	komedor
Dining-table	mesa(f)de comedor	mesa de komedor

Dinner-knife	cuchillo(m)grande	koochillo graande
Dinner-plate	plato(m)grande	plaato graande
Dinner-trolley	carrito(m)de la comida	karrito de la-komida
Dishwasher	lavaplatos(m)	lavaplaatos
Door	puerta(f)	pooerta
Doorbell	timbre(m)	timbre
Doorchain	cadena(f)de la puerta	kadena de la-pooerta
Doorframe	marco(m)de la puerta	maarko de la-pooerta
Doormat	felpudo(m)	felpoodo
Doorstep	umbral(m)	oombraal
Drain	desaguadero(m)	desagooadero
Drawer	cajón(m)	kakhón
Drawing-room	salón(m)	saalón
Dressing-table	tocador(m)	tokador
Eaves	alero(m)	aalero
Family size packet	paqute(m)familiar	pakete familiaar
Fan	ventilador(m)	ventilaador
Finger bowl	lavafrutas(m)	lavafrutas
Floor	suello(m)	suello
Fork	tenedor(m)	tenedor
Foundation	fundación(f)	fundathión
Frying pan	sartén(f)	sartén
Funnel	embudo(m)	embudo
Gallery	galeria(f)	gaalería
Gas-cooker	cocina(f)de gas	kothina de gaas
Gas-cylinder	bombona(f)de gas	bombona de gaas
Glass	vaso(m)	vaso
Grate	parilla(f) de hogar	parilla de ogar

Hall	sala(f)	saala
Hand wash	lavar(v)a mano	lavar a mano
Hearth	hogar(m)	ogaar
House	casa(f)	kasa
Inkpot	tintero(m)	tintero
Jar	tarro(m)	tarro
Jug	jarro(m)	kharro
Key	llave(f)	llave
Kitchen	cocina(f)	kothina
Knife	cuchillo(m)	kuchillo
Knife(folding)	navaja(f)	navakha
Knife and fork	cubierto(m)	koobierto
Ladle	cacillo(m)	kathillo
Lamp	lámpara(f)	lámpara
Lid	tapa(f)	tapa
Lock	cerradura(f)	therradura
Mat	estera(f)	estera
Match	fósforo(m)	fósforo
Mattress	colchón(m)	kolchón
Medicine cabinet	botiquín(m)	botikín
Microwave oven	horno(m)de microonda	orno de-mikroonda
Mug	taza(f)	tatha
Mug(beer)	jarro(m)	kharro
Needle	aguja(f)	agukha
Niche	nicho(m)	nicho
Oven	horno(m)	orno
Peeler	mondador(m)	mondador
Peeler(electric)	pelacables(m)	pelakables
Peephole	mirilla(f)	mirilla
Peg	clavija(f)	klavikha

Plaster	yeso(m)	yeso
Plate	plato(m)	plaato
Plinth	plinto(m)	plinto
Portico	pórtico(m)	portico
Quilt	colcha(f)	kolcha
Radio	radio(f)	radio
Rafter	par(m)	paar
Railing	baranda(f)	baraanda
Recordplayer	tocadiscos(m)	tokadiskos
Refrigerator	refrigerador(m)	refrikheraador
Rocking-chair	mecedora(f)	methedora
Roof	techo(m)	techo
Room	cuarto(m)	kuarto
Rope	cuerda(f)	kuerda
Sack	saco(m)	sako
Safe	cámara(f) de acorazada	kámara de-akorathada
Saucepan	cazo(m)	katho
Shed	alpende(m)	aalpende
Shower	ducha(f)	ducha
Sieve	tamiz(m)	tamith
Sink(kitchen)	fregadero(m)	fregaadero
Sofa	sofá(m)	sofá
Sofa-bed	sofá-cama(m)	sofá-kama
Spitton	escupidera(f)	eskupidera
Spoon	cuchara(f)	kuchara
Stair	escalón(m)	eskalón
Steeple	aguja(f)	aagukha
Stick	palo(m)	palo
Stone	piedra(f)	piedra
Stool	escabel(m)	eskabel

Storey	piso(m)	piso
Stove	hornillo(m)	ornillo
String	cuerda(f)	kuerda
Studio apartment	estudio(m)	estudio
Table	mesa(f)	mesa
Table cloth	mantel(m)	mantel
Tape-recorder	magnetofón(m)	magnetofón
Teacloth	paño(m)de cocina	panio de kothina
Tea-cosy	cubretetera(f)	kubretetera
Teacup	taza(f)para té	tatha para té
Teakettle	tetera(f)	tetera
Television	televisión(f)	televisión
Thimble	dedal(m)	dedaal
Tile	teja(f)	tekha
Tissue paper	papel(m) de seda	papel de seda
Toaster	tostadora(f)	tostadora
Tongs	tenazas(fpl)	tenaathaas
Torch	lámpara(f)de bolsillo	lámpara de-bolsillo
Tray	bandeja(f)	bandekha
Tumbler	caída(f)	kaída
Umbrella	paraguas(m)	paraguas
Urinal	urinario(m)	oorinaario
Vase	jarrón(m)	kharrón
Wall	papel(m)pintado	papel pintaado
Wall-painting	pintura(f)mural	pintura mooral
Washing-machine	lavadora(f)	lavadora
Washing-powder	jabon(m)en polvo	khabon en polvo
Whitewash	jalbegue(m)	khalbegay
Wick	mecha(f)	mecha
Window	ventana(f)	ventaana

Chapter 8

Toiletries
Articulos De Tocador

English	Spanish	Pronunciation
Brush	cepillo(m)	thepillo
Dandruff shampoo	champu(m)anticaspa	champu antikaspa
Deodarant	desodorante(m)	desodoraante
Mouth-wash	enjuague(m)	enkhuagay
Perfume	perfume(m)	perfume
Razor	navaja(f)	navakha
Razor(electric)	rasuradora(f)	rasuradora
Roll-on deodorant	bola(f)desodorante	bola desodoraante
Scissors	tijeras(fpl)	tikheraas
Shampoo	champu(m)	champu
Shaving-brush	brocha(f)de afeitar	brocha de afeitar
Shaving-cream	crema(f)de afeitar	krema de afeitaar
Soap	jabon(m)	khabon
Sunblock	crema(f)solar	krema solaar
Suntan lotion	bronceador(m)	brontheador
Tissue paper	papel(m)de seda	papel de seda
Toothbrush	cepillo(m)de dientes	thepillo de dientes
Toothpaste	pasta(f) dentrifica	pasta dentrifika
Tooth-powder	polvos(mpl) dentrificos	polvos dentrifikos
Towel	toalla(f)	toalla
Underpants	calzoncillos(mpl)	kalthonthillos
Undergarments	ropa(f)interior	ropa interior

Chapter 9

School
Colegio

I am studying business.
Estudio comercio.
Estoodio komerthio.

Iam studying at college.
Estudio en el instituto.
Estoodio en l institooto.

What grade are you in?
¿En qué curso estás?
¿En ké koorso estás?

Do you like school?
¿Te gusta el colegio?
¿Te goosta l kolekhio?

What do you do after school?
¿Qué haces después del colegio?
¿Ké athes despooéa del kolekhio?

Is there a crèche here?
¿Hay una guardería aquí?
¿Ay oona gooardería akí?

Where is the playground?
¿Dónde está el parque infantil?
¿Dónde está l parke infantil?

Are there swings in the school?
¿Hay columpios en el colegio?
¿Ay koloompios en l kolegio?

And a slide too?
¿Y un tobogán también?
¿Y oon tobogáan también?

Chapter 10

Clothing
Ropa

English	Spanish	Pronunciation
Apron	delantal(m)	delantaal
Bathing-cap	gorro(m)de baño	gorro de banio
Bathing-suit	traje(m)de baño	trakhe de banio
Bathrobe	albornoz(m)	albornoth
Belt	cinturón(m)	thinturón
Bikini	bikini(m)	bikini
Blanket	manta(f)	manta
Blouse	blusa(f)	blusa
Blue jeans	tejanos(mpl)	tekhanos
Bra	sostén(m)	sostén
Brocada	brocado(m)	brokado
Bodice	corpiño(m)	korpinio
Border	orla(f)	orla
Button	botón(m)	botón
Boots	botas(fpl)	botas
Bra	sostén(m)	sostén
Canvas	lona(f)	lona
Cap	gorra(f)	gorra
Cardigan	rebeca(f)	rebeka
Cashmere	cachemira(f)	kachemira
Chintz	cretona(f)	kretona
Cloak	capa(f)	kapa
Cloth	tela(f)	tela

Coat	chaqueta(f)	chaketa
Corduroy	pana(f)	pana
Corduroys	pantalones(mpl)de pana	pantaalones de-pana
Corset	faja(f)	fakha
Damask	damasco(m)	damasko
Darning	cosas(fpl) por zurcir	kosas por zurthir
Dress	vestido(m)	vestido
Dressing-gown(lady's)	bata(f)	bata
Dressing-gown(man's)	batín(m)	batín
Flannel	franela(f)	franela
Gloves	guantes(fpl)	guantes
Handkerchief	pañuelo(m)	paniuelo
Hat	sombrero(m)	sombrero
Jacket	chaqueta(f)	chaketa
Jersey	jersey	khersey
Knitted	de punto	de punto
Knitting wool	lana(f)para labores	lana para labores
Lace	encaje(m)	enkakhe
Leather-jacket	cazadora(f)de piel	kathadora de piel
Lingerie	ropa(f)interior	ropa interior
Lining	forro(m)	forro
Muffler	bufanda(f)	bufanda
Napkin	servilleta(f)	servilleta
Nightgown	camisón(m)de noche	kamisón de noche
Pajamas	pijama	pikhama
Pants	calzoncillos	kalthonthillos
Panties	bragas(fpl)	bragas
Pantsuit	traje(m)de chaqueta	trakhe de chaketa
Parka	anorak(m)	anoraak

Petticoat	enaguas(fpl)	enaguas
Pocket	bolsillo(m)	bolsillo
Polyester	poliéster(m)	poliéster
Raincoat	impermeable(m)	impermeable
Sackcloth	tela(f)de saco	tela de saako
Scarf	pañuelo(m)	paniuelo
Serge	sarga(f)	saarga
Shawl	chal(m)	chal
Shirt	camisa(f)	kamisa
Skirt	falda(f)	falda
Sleeve	manga(f)	maanga
Slip	combinación(f)	kombinathión
Sportswear	ropa(f)de deporte	ropa de deporte
Stitching	puntadas(fpl)	puntaadaas
Stocking	media(f)	media
Stole	estola(f)	estola
Suit(man's)	traje(m)	trakhe
Suit(woman's)	traje(m)de chaqueta	trakhe de chaketa
Thread	hilo(m)	eelo
Tie	corbata(f)	korbaata
Tie-clip	pinza(f)de corbata	pintha de korbaata
Tunic	túnica(f)	túnika
Towel	toalla(f)	toalla
Trousers	pantalones(mpl)	paantaalones
Turban	turbante(m)	turbaante
Underpants	calzoncillos(mpl)	kalthonthillos
Veil	velo(m)	velo
Worsted	estambre(m)	estaambre
Waistcoat	chaleco(m)	chaleko
Yarn	hilo(m)	eelo

Chapter 11

Numbers
Numeros

	English	Spanish	Pronounciation
1.	One	uno(m) una(f)	uno una
2.	Two	dos	dos
3.	Three	tres	tres
4.	Four	cuatro	kuatro
5.	Five	cinco	cinko
6.	Six	seis	seis
7.	Seven	siete	siete
8.	Eight	ocho	ocho
9.	Nine	nueve	nueve
10.	Ten	diez	diez
11.	Eleven	once	once
12.	Twelve	doce	doce
13.	Thirteen	trece	trece
14.	Fourteen	catorce	katorce
15.	Fifteen	quince	kince
16.	Sixteen	dieciséis	dieciséis
17.	Seventeen	diecisiete	diecisiete
18.	Eighteen	dieciocho	dieciocho
19.	Nineteen	diecinueve	diecinueve
20.	Twenty	veinte	veinte
21.	Twentyone	veintiuno	veintiuno
22.	Twentytwo	veintidós	veintidós
23.	Twentythree	veintitrés	veintitrés
24.	Twentyfour	veinticuatro	veintikuatro

25.	Twentyfive	veinticinco	veintithinko
26.	Twentysix	veintiseis	veintiseis
27.	Twentyseven	veintisiete	veintisiete
28.	Twentyeight	veintiocho	veintiocho
29.	Twentynine	veintinueve	veintinooeve
30.	Thirty	treinta	treinta
31.	Thirtyone	treinta y uno	treinta y uno
32.	Thirtytwo	treinta y dos	treinta y dos
33.	Thirtythree	treinta y tres	treinta y tres
34.	Thirtyfour	treinta y cuatro	treinta y kuatro
35.	Thirtyfive	treinta y cinco	treinta y thinko
36.	Thirtysix	treinta y seis	treinta y sies
37.	Thirtyseven	treinta y siete	treinta y siete
38.	Thirtyeight	treinta y ocho	treinta y ocho
39.	Thirtynine	treinta y nueve	treinta y nooeve
40.	Forty	cuarenta	kuarenta
41.	Fortyone	cuarenta y uno	kuarenta y oono
42.	Fortytwo	cuarenta y dos	kuarenta y dos
43.	Fortythree	cuarenta y tres	kuarenta y tres
44.	Fortyfour	cuarenta y cuatro	kuarenta y kuatro
45.	Fortyfive	cuarenta y cinco	kuarenta y thinko
46.	Fortysix	cuarenta y seis	kuarenta y seis
47.	Fortyseven	cuarenta y siete	kuarenta y siete
48.	Fortyeight	cuarenta y ocho	kuarenta y ocho
49.	Fortynine	cuarenta y nueve	kuarenta y nooeve
50.	Fifty	cincuenta	thinkuenta
51.	Fiftyone	cincuenta y uno	thinkuenta y oono
52.	Fiftytwo	cincuenta y dos	thinkuenta y dos
53.	Fiftythree	cincienta y tres	thinkuenta y tres
54.	Fiftyfour	cincuenta y cuatro	thinkuenta y kuatro

55.	Fiftyfive	cicuenta y cinco	thinkuenta y thinko
56.	Fiftysix	cincuenta y seis	thinkuenta y seis
57.	Fiftyseven	cincuenta y siete	thinkuenta y siete
58.	Fiftyeight	cincuenta y ocho	thinkuenta y ocho
59	Fiftynine	cincuenta y nueve	thinkuenta y- nooeve
60.	Sixty	sesenta	sesenta
61.	Sixtyone	sesenta y uno	sesenta y oono
62.	Sixtytwo	sesenta y dos	sesenta y dos
63.	Sixtythree	sesenta y tres	sesenta y tres
64.	Sixtyfour	sesenta y cuatro	sesenta y kuatro
65.	Sixtyfive	sesenta y cinco	sesenta y thinko
66.	Sixtysix	sesenta y seis	sesenta y seis
67.	Sixtyseven	sesenta y siete	sesenta y siete
68.	Sixtyeight	sesenta y ocho	sesenta y ocho
69.	Sixtynine	sesenta y nueve	sesenta y nooeve
70.	Seventy	setenta	setenta
71.	Seventyone	sestenta y uno	setenta y oono
72.	Seventytwo	setenta y dos	setenta y dos
73.	Seventythree	setenta y tres	setenta y tres
74.	Seventyfour	setenta y cuatro	setenta y kuatro
75.	Seventyfive	setenta y cinco	setenta y thinko
76.	Seventysix	setenta y seis	setenta y seis
77.	Seventyseven	setenta y siete	setenta y siete
78.	Seventyeight	setenta y ocho	setenta y ocho
79.	Seventynine	setenta y nueve	setenta y nooeve
80.	Eighty	ochenta	ochenta
81.	Eightyone	ochenta y uno	ochenta y oono
82.	Eightytwo	ochenta y dos	ochenta y dos
83.	Eightythree	ochenta y tres	ochenta y tres
84.	Eightyfour	ochenta y cuatro	ochenta y kuatro

85.	Eightyfive	ochenta y cinco	ochenta y thinko
86.	Eightysix	ochenta y seis	ochenta y seis
87.	Eightyseven	ochenta y siete	ochenta y siete
88.	Eightyeight	ochenta y ocho	ochenta y ocho
89.	Eightynine	ochenta y nueve	ochenta y nooeve
90.	Ninety	noventa	noventa
91.	Ninetyone	noventa y uno	noventa y oono
92.	Ninetytwo	noventa y dos	noventa y dos
93.	Ninetythree	noventa y tres	noventa y tres
94.	Ninetyfour	noventa y cuatro	noventa y kuatro
95.	Ninetyfive	noventa y cinco	noventa y thinko
96.	Ninetysix	noventa y seis	noventa y seis
97.	Ninetyseven	noventa y siete	noventa y siete
98.	Ninetyeight	noventa y ocho	noventa y ocho
99.	Ninetynine	noventa y nueve	noventa y nooeve
100.	Hundred	cien	thien
101.	Hundredone	ciento uno	ciento uno
200.	Twohundred	doscientos(m) doscientas(f)	doscientos doscientas
1000.	Thousand	mil	mil
1002.	Thousand-and two	mil dos	mil dos
2000.	Two thou-sand	dos mil	dos mil
10000.	Ten tho-usand	diez mil	diez mil
100000.	Hundred-thousand	cien mil	cien mil
1000000.	Million	un millón	un millón

Chapter 12

Money & Currency Exchange
Moneda & Cambio

English	Spanish	Pronounciation
Currency	moneda(f)	moneda
Currency market	mercado(m)monetario	merkado monetario
Currency note	pagaré(m)fiscal	pagaré fiskaal
Currency restrictions	restricciones(fpl)-monetarias	restrikthiones-monetaarias
Currency unit	unidad(f)-monetaria	oonidad-monetaaria
Dollar bill	billete(m)de un dólar	billete de un dólaar
Dollar rate	cambio(m)de dólar	kambio de dólaar
Dollar sign	signo(m)del dólar	signo del dólaar
Foreign exchange	divisas(fpl)	divisas
Exchange rate	tipo de cambio	tipo de kambio
Traveller's cheque	cheque de viaje	cheke de viakhe

Where can I change some money?
¿Dónde podría cambiar unos billetes?
¿Dónde podría kambiar unos billetes?

What is the exchange rate?
¿Cuál es el tipo de cambio?
¿Kuál es l tipo de kambio?

I am out of cash.
Estoy sin blanca.
Estoy sin blanka.

I haven't any cash on me.
No llevo dinero conmigo.
No llevo dinero konmigo.

What's the charge for that?
¿Cuánto hay que pagar por eso?
¿Kuánto ay ke pagar por eso?

You may keep the change.
Quédese con la vuelta.
Kédese kon la vooelta.

I would like to change money .
Me gustaría cambiar dinero.
Me goostaría kambiar dinero.

I would like to change a traveller's cheque.
Me gustaría cambiar un cheque de viajero.
Me goostaría kambiar oon cheke de viakhero.

I would like to change 5.000 rupees into euros.
Querría cambiar 5,000 rupias en euros.
Kerría kambiar 5,000 roopias en eooros.

Where is the nearest ATM?
¿Dónde está el cajero automático más cercano?
¿Dónde está l kakhero aootamátiko más therkano?

Can I use my credit card to withdraw money?
¿Puedo usar mi tarjeta de crédito para sacar dinero?
¿Pooedo oosar mi tarkheta de krédito para sakar dinero?

Can I have some coins/tokens?
¿Me podía dar monedas/fichas?
¿Me podía dar monedas/fichas?

Chapter 13

Time
Tiempo

English	Spanish	Pronounciation
Afternoon	tarde(f)	tarde
A quarter of- An hour	un cuarto de hora	un kuarto de ora
Anniversary	aniversario(m)	aniversario
At times	a veces	a vethes
A while	un rato	oon rato
Century	siglo(m)	siglo
Dawn	amanecer(m)	amanether
Day	día(m)	día
Day-to-day	cotidiano	kotidiano
Decade	decenio(m)	dethenio
Evening	noche(f)	noche
Fortnight	quincena(f)	kinthena
Golden jubilee	quincuagésimo aniver-sario	kinkuakhésimo-aniversario
Hour	hora(f)	la ora
Late	tarde	tarde
Leap year	año(m)bisieto	anio bisieto
Midday	mediodía(m)	mediodía
Midnight	medianoche(f)	medianoche
Minute	minuto(m)	minuto
Morning	mañana(f)	maniana
New year	año(m) nuevo	anio nuevo
New year's eve	noche(f)vieja	noche vieja

Period	período(m)	período
Second	segundo (m)	segundo
Silver jubilee	vigésimo quinto-aniversario	vikhésimo-aniversario
Sometimes	a veces	a vethes
Time	tiempo(m)	tiempo

PRESENT

Now	ahora	aora
Nowadays	hoy día	oy día
Right now	ahora mismo	aọra mismo
This afternoon	esta tarde	esta tarde
This month	este mes	este mes
This morning	esta mañana	esta maniana
This week	esta semana	esta semana
This year	este año	este anio
Today	hoy(m)	oy
Tonight	esta noche	esta noche

PAST

Day before-Yesterday	anteayer	anteayer
Last month	el mes pasado	l mes pasaado
Last night	anoche	anoche
Last time	última vez(f)	última veth
Last week	la semana pasada	la semaana pasaada
Last year	el año pasado	l anio pasaado
Since	desde	desde
The year before	año(m)pasado	anio pasado
Two days ago.	hace dos días	athe dos días

Yesterday	ayer(m)	ayer
Yesterday afternoon	ayer por la tarde	ayer por la tarde
Yesterday evening	ayer por la noche	ayer por la noche
Yesterday morning	ayer por la mañana	ayer por la maniana

FUTURE

Day after - Tomorrow	pasado mañana	pasado maniana
In a month	un mes	oon mes
In an hour	dentro de una hora	dentro de oona-ora
In five minutes	dentro de cinco minutos	dentro de thinko-minootos
In two days	dentro de dos días	dentro de dos días
Next month	el mes que viene	l mes ke viene
Next week	la semana que viene	la semaana ke-viene
Next year	el año que viene	l anio ke viene
Tomorrow	mañana(f)	maniana
Tomorrow afternoon	mañana por la tarde	maniana por la tarde
Tomorrow evening	mañana por la noche	maniana por la-noche
Tomorrow morning	mañana por la mañana	maniana por la-maniana
Until	hasta	asta

*The verb Ser and the feminine article La are used to tell time wherever "it's..." is used in english in present tense. For time in past and future tense the same rule applies except for the fact that "era", "eran" and "será", "serán" are used respectively.

-What is the time?
¿qué hora es?
¿ké ora es?

-It's 1 o'clock.
Es la una. es (for 1 or less) + la + time
Es la oona

-It's 2 o'clock
Son las dos. son (for 2 or more) + las + time
Son las dos.

-It's half-past 9.
Son las nueve y media.(literally this means nine and half. So denote 'past' by 'y' which means 'and')
Son las nooeve y media.

-It's quarter past 8
Son las ocho y cuarto (quarter = cuarto)
Son las ocho y kuarto.

-It's quarter to 6
Son las seis menos cuarto
Son las seis menos kuarto.

-It's 10 to 7.
Son las siete menos diez.(literally this means it is seven o'clock minus 10 minutes.So denote 'to' by 'menos' which implies minus the minutes left)
Son laas siete menos dieth.

-At 10 a.m.
A las diez de la mañana.
A laas dieth de la maniana.

-At 3 p.m. sharp.
A las tres en punto de la tarde.
A laas tres en poonto de la taarde.

Note : a.m. is denoted by 'de la mañana'and p.m. by 'de la tarde'.

-3(three) hours 20 (twenty) minutes and 10 (ten) seconds
3 (tres) horas 20 (veinte) minutos and 10 (diez) segundos
3 (tres)oras 20 (veinte) minootos and 10 (diez) segoondos

-The train\bus leaves at 16.35.
El tren\autobús sale a las dieciséis treinta y cinco.
El tren\autoboos sale a las diethiséis treinta y thinko.

-Until 10 o'clock
Hasta las diez
Asta las dieth.

-'open \ closed from . . . to. . .'
'abierto\cerrado de . . . . a. . .'
'abierto\therrado de. . .a. . .'

-It's late.
Es tarde.
Es tarde.

Chapter 14

Week
Semana

English	Spanish	Pronunciation
Monday	el lunes	l lunes
Tuesday	el martes*	l martes
Wednesday	el miércoles	l miérkoles
Thursday	el jueves	l khueves
Friday	el viernes	l viernes
Saturday	el sábado	l sábado
Sunday	el domingo	l domingo

Note : names of days are not capitalized and they usually carry a masculine article(un, el) except after the verb ser.E.g

-Tomorrow is friday.
Mañana es viernes
Maniana es viernes

-On Monday
El lunes
L loones

-On Tuesdays
Los martes
Los maartes.

*According to Spanish superstiuon Tuesday is an unlucky day, even more so if it falls on the 13th of the month. As the proverb goes, "En martes, ni te cases ni te embarques".

Chapter 15

Months
Meses

English	Spanish	Pronunciation
January	enero(m)	enero
February	febrero(m)	febrero
March	marzo(m)	martho
April	abril(m)	abril
May	mayo(m)	mayo
June	junio(m)	khunio
July	julio(m)	khulio
August	agosto(m)	agosto
September	setiembre(m)	setiembre
October	octubre(m)	oktubre
November	noviembre(m)	noviembre
December	diciembre(m)	dithiembre

Chapter 16

Date
Fecha

What is the date today?
¿Qué día es hoy?
¿Ké día es oy?

Today's the 23rd March.
Hoy es el veintitrés de marzo.
Oy es l veintitrés de martho.

On the 3rd of this month/of next month.
El 3 de este mes /próximo mes
L 3 de este mes/próximo mes.

Until 6th May
Hasta 6 de mayo.
Asta 6 de mayo.

Chapter 17

Hobbies
Pasatiempos

English	Spanish	Pronunciation
Cooking	cocinar	kothinar
Dancing	ir a bailar	ir a bailar
Gardening	jardinería	khardinería
Hiking	el excursionismo	l exkoorsionismo
Pub crawls	ir de bar en bar	ir de bar en bar
Reading	leer	leer
Shopping	ir de compras	ir de kompras
Socialising	salir	saalir
Sport	el deporte	l deporte
Travelling	viajar	viakhar

Do you like traveling?
¿Te gusta viajar?
¿Te goosta viakhar?

Do you like to play an instrument?
¿Te gusta tocar algún instrumento?
¿Te goosta tokar algoon instroomento?

Do you like to sing?
¿Te gusta cantar?
¿Te goosta kantar?

Do you like to listen to music?
¿Te gusta escuchar música?
¿Te goosta eskuchar moosika?

Do you like to see movies?
¿Te gusta ver películas?
¿Te goosta ver pelíkulas?

Do you like to go to concerts?
¿Te gusta ir a conciertos?
¿Te goosta ir a konthiertos?
¿Te goosta ir a konthiertos?

What music do you like?
¿Qué música te gusta?
¿Ké moosika te goosta?

Chapter 18

Relatioships
Relaciones

English	Spanish	Pronunciation
Adopted	Adoptivo	Adoptivo
Aunt	Tía	Tía
Boyfriend	Amigo(m)	Aamigo
Bride	Novia(f)	Novia
Bridegroom	Novio(m)	Novio
Brother	Hermano(m)	Ermaano
Brother-in-law	Cuñado(m)	Kuniado
Cousin	Primo(m)	Primo
Cousin	Prima(f)	Prima
Daughter	Hija(f)	Ikha
Daughter-in-law	Nuera(f)	Nooera
Elder brother	Hermano(m)mayor	Ermaano mayor
Elder sister	Hermana(f)mayor	Ermaana mayor
Family	Familia(f)	Faamilia
Father	Padre(m)	Paadre
Father-in-law	Suegro(m)	Sooegro
Fiancé	Novio(m)	Novio
Fiancée	Novia(f)	Novia
Girlfriend	Amiga(f)	Aamiga
Grandchildren	Nietos(mpl)	Nietos
Granddaughter	Nieta(f)	Nieta
Grandparents	Abuelos(mpl)	Aabooelos
Grandson	Nieto(m)	Nieto
Guest	Convidado(m/f)	Konvidado

Host	Huésped(m/f)	Ooésped
Husband	Marido(m)	Maarido
Mother	Madre(f)	Maadre
Mother-in-law	Suegra(f)	Sooegra
Neighbour	Vecino(m/f)	Vethino
Nephew	Sobrino(m)	Sobrino
Niece	Sobrina(f)	Sobrina
Parents	Padres(mpl)	Padres
Relative	Pariente(m)	Paariente
Sister	Hermana(f)	Ermana
Son	Hijo(m)	Ikho
Son-in-law	Yerno(m)	Yerno
Spouse	Cónyuge(m,f)	Kónyukhe
Twin brother	Hermano(m)gemelo	Ermaano khemelo
Twin sister	Hermana(f)gemela	Ermaana khemela
Uncle	Tío(m)	Tío
Wedding	Boda(f)	Boda
Widow	Viuda(f)	Viuda
Widower	Viudo(m)	Viudo
Wife	Esposa(f)	Esposa
Younger brother	Hermano(m)menor	Ermaano menor
Younger sister	Hermana(f)menor	Ermaana menor

Chapter 19

Sports
Deportes

English	Spanish	Pronunciation
Abseiling	rappel(m)	rappel
Ace	ace(m)	athc
Athlete	atleta(m,f)	atleta
Athletics	atletismo(m)	atletismo
Badminton	bádminton	bádminton
Ball	bola(f)	bola
Basketball	baloncesto(m)	balonthesto
Bat	maza(f)	matha
Bungy-jumping	puenting	pooenting
Bullfight	corrida(f)de toros	korrida de toros
Card-game	juego(m)de cartas	khuego de kartas
Caving	espeleología(f)	espeleolokhía
Champion	campeón	kampeón
Championship	campeonato(m)	kampeonato
Coach	entrenador(m)	entrenador
Corner	saque(m)de esquina	sake de eskina
Cricket	cricket(m)	cricket
Cricketer	criquetero(m)	kriketero
Cycling	ciclismo	thiklismo
Defeat	derrota(f)	derrota
Fault	falta(f)	faalta
Free kick	tiro(m)libre	tiro libre
Football	fútbol(m)	footbol

Game	deporte(m)	deporte
Game fishing	pesca(f)deportiva	peska deportiva
Goal	gol(m)	gol
Goal keeper	portero(m)portera(f)	portero
Golf	golf(m)	golf
Group	grupo(m)	grupo
Hockey	hockey(m)	hockey
Judo	judo(m)	khudo
Karate	karate(m)	karate
Ludo	ludo(m)	ludo
Match	partido(m)	partido
Mountain biking	ciclismo(m)de montaña	thiklismo de-montania
Offside	fuera de juego	fooera de khuego
Penalty	penalty(m)	penalty
Pass	pase	pase
Player	jugador(m)jugadora(f)	khugador, khugadora
Playground	patio(m)	patio
Play doubles	jugar dobles	khugar dobles
Racket	raqueta(f)	raketa
Rock-climbing	escalada(f)	eskalada
Serve	saque(m)	sake
Snakes&ladders	juego(m)de escaleras-y serpientes	khuego de eska-leras e serpientes
Sportsman	deportista(m)	deporteesta
SStriker	delantero(m)	delaantero
Surfboard	tabla(f)de surf	tabla de soorf
Surfing	surf(m)	soorf
Swimmer	nadador(m)	nadador

Swimming	natación(f)	natathión
Team	eqipo(m)	ekipo
Tennis	tenis(m)	tennis
Tennis-court	pista(f)de tennis	pista de tenis
Victory	triunfo(m)	triunfo
Volleyball	balonvolea(m)	balonvolea
Water-skis	esquís(mpl)acuáticos	eskís akuátikos
Winner	ganador(m)	ganador
Wrestling	lucha(f)	loocha

Do you like sport?
¿Te gustan los deportes?
¿Te goostan los deportes?

Yes,very much.
Me encantan.
Me enkantan.

Not really.
En realidad,no mucho.
En realidad,no moocho.

Would you like to go to a cricket match?
¿Te gustaría ir a un partido de cricket?
¿Te goostaría ir a oon partido de kriket?

What is the score now?
¿Cómo van ahora?
¿Kómo van aora?

It's a draw/love.
Empatados/cero.
Empatados/thero.

It's a match-point.
Match-point.
Match-point.

How much time is left?
¿Cuánto tiempo queda de partido?
¿Kuánto tiempo keda de partido?

What sport do you play?
¿Qué deporte practicas?
¿Ké deporte praktikas?

I play . . .
Practico. . .
Praktiko. . .

Who's your favourite sportsperson?
¿Quién es tu deportista favorito/a?
¿Kién es tu deportista favorito/a?

I follow. . .
Soy aficionado/a al. . .
Soy afithionado/a al. . .

I like watching.
Me gusta mirar.
Me goosta mirar.

Which is your favourite team?
¿Cuál es tu equipo favorito?
¿Kuál es tu ekipo favorito?

Who plays for Real Madrid?
¿Quién juega en el Real Madrid?
¿Kién khuega en l Real Madrid?

Which team is at the top of the league?
¿Qué equipo está en primera posición en la liga?
¿Ké ekipo está en primera posithión en la liga?

Which team are you supporting?
¿Con qué equipo vas?
¿Kon ké ekipo vas?

That was a great match!
¡Ese partido fue cojonudo!
¡Ese partido fooe kokhonoodo!

Do you want to play?
¿Quieres jugar?
¿Kieres khugar?

Can I join in?
¿Puede jugar?
¿Pooede khugar?

Can I hire a racquet?
¿Es posible alquilar una raqueta?
¿Es posible alkilar oona raketa?

What's the charge per day?
¿Cuánto cobran por día?
¿Kuánto kobran por día?

What's the charge per hour?
¿Cuánto cobran por hora?
¿Kuánto kobran por ora?

I would like to go scuba diving.
Me gustaría hacer submarinismo.
Me goostaría ather soobmarinismo.

I would like to learn to dive.
Me gustaría aprender a bucear.
Me goostaría aprender boothear.

Where are some good diving sites?
¿Dónde hay buenos lugares para bucear?
¿Dónde ay booenos loogares para boothear?

Where can I hire diving equipment?
¿Dónde se puede alquilar equipo de buceo?
¿Dónde se pooede alkilar ekipo bootheo?

Are you sure this is safe?
¿De verdad que esto es seguro?
¿De verdad ke esto es segooro?

Part-III
Food & Health

Chapter 1

Foodstuff
Comestibles

English	Spanish	Pronunciation
Appetite	Apetito(m)	Apetito
Appetizer	Tapa(f)	Taapa
Apple-pie	Tarta(f)de manzanas	Tarta de-manthanas
Apple-sauce	Compota(f)de manzanas	Kompota de manthanas
Apple-tart	Tarta(f)de manzanas	Tarta de manthanas
Baked beans	Judías(fpl)en salsa de tomate	Khudías en salsa de tomate
Baked potatoes	Patatas(fpl)al horno	Patatas al orno
Bean curd	Tofu(m)	Tofu
Beansprouts	Brotes(mpl)de soja	Brotes de sokha
Beanstalk	Judía(f)	Khudía
Beef	Carne de vaca(F)	Karne de vaka
Biscuit	Galleta(f)	Galleta
Boiled egg	Huevo(m) hervido	Uevo ervido
Bread	Pan(M)	Paan
Bread and butter	Pan(m)con mantequilla	Paan manteklla
Bread crumbs	Pan(m)rallado	Paan rallado

Breadfruit	Fruto(m)del pan	Frooto del paan
Breakfast	Desayuno(m)	Desayouno
Brown bread	Pan(m)moreno	Paan moreno
Brown egg	Huevo(m)moreno	Uevo moreno
Buffet lunch	Buffet(m)libre	Buffet libre
Buffet meal	Comida(f)buffet	Komida buffet
Buffet supper	Cena(f)fría	Thena fría
Butter	Mantequilla(f)	Mantekilla
Cake	Pastel(m)	Pastel
Candy	Azúcar(m)cande	Athúkar kande
Cheddar	Queso(m)cheddar	Keso cheddar
Cheese	Queso(M)	Keso
Cheeseburger	Hamburguesa(f)- con queso	Amboorgaysa kon keso
Cheesecake	Quesadilla(f)	Kesadilla
Cheesedish	Quesera(f)	Kesera
Chicken	Pollo(m)	Pollo
Chili sauce	Salsa(f)de ají	Saalsa de akhí
Chocolate biscuit	Galleta(f)de chocolate	Galleta de- chokolaate
Chop	Chuleta(f)	Chuleta
Cocktail sausage	Salchichita(f)de aperitivo	Salchichita de- aperitivo
Coffee cake	Pastel(m)de café	Pastel de kafé
Cold meat	Fiambre(m)	Fiaambre
Continental breakfast	Desayuno(m)continental	Desayouno- kontinentaal
Cookie	Galleta(f)	Galleta
Corn bread	Pan(m)de maíz	Paan de maíth
Cornflakes	Copos(mpl)de maíz	Kopos de maaíth
Cornflour	Harina(f)de maíz	Arina de maíth

Corn meal	Harina(f)de maíz	Arina de maíth
Cottage cheese	Requesón(m)	Rekesón
Crab meat	Carne(f)de cangrejo	Karne de kangrekho
Cracker	Galleta(f)para queso	Galleta para keso
Cream cake	Pastel(m)de nata	Pastel de naata
Cream cheese	Requesón(m)	Rekesón
Cream cracker	Galleta(f)de soda	Galleta de soda
Curd	Cuajada(f)	Kuakhada
Curry	Curry(m)	Kurry
Curry powder	Polvo(m)de curry	Polvo de curry
Custard	Natillas(fpl)	Natillas
Custard tart	Pastel(m)de crema	Pastel de krema
Dairy butter	Mantequilla(f)de granja	Mantekilla de-grankha
Dessert	Postre(m)	Postre
Dessert apple	Manzana(f)para-repostería	Manthana de-repostería
Diet	Dieta(f)	Dieta
Dinner	Cena(f)	Thena
Dish	Plato(m)	Plaato
Drumstick	Pierna(f)de pavo	Pierna de paavo
Egg	Huevo(m)	Uevo
Egg white	Clara(f)de huevo	Klara de uevo
Egg yolk	Yema(f)de huevo	Yemo de uevo
Fish	Pescado(m)	Peskaado
Flour	Harina(f)	Arinaa
French bread	Pan(m)francés	Paan franthés
French fries	Patatas(f) fritas	Pataataas fritaas
French loaf	Barra(f)de pan-francés	Barra de paan-franthés

French pastry	Pastelito(m)	Paastelito
French toast	Torrija(f)	Torrikha
Fried egg	Huevo(m)frito	Uevo frito
Fried fish	Pescado(m)frito	Peskaado frito
Fritter	Churro(m)	Churro
Fruit-cake	Tarta(f)de frutas	Taarta de frootas
Fruit-salad	Macedonia(f)de frutas	Mathedonia de-frootaas
Fruit-salts	Sal(f)de frutas	Saal de frootaas
Garlic salt	Sal(f)de ajo	Saal de akho
Garlic sausage	Salchicha(f)de ajo	Saalchicha de akho
Ginger bread	Pan(m)de jenjibre	Paan de-khenkhibre
Goat's cheese	Queso(m)de cabra	Keso de kabra
Green salad	Ensalada(f)	Ensaalada
Ham	Jamón(m)	Khamón
Hamburger	Hamburguesa(f)	Amboorgaysa
High-fibre diet	Dieta(f)rica en fibra	Dieta rika en fibra
High-protein diet	Dieta(f)rika en proteínas	Dieta rika en-proteínaas
Honey	Miel(f)	Miel
Hotdog	Perrito(m)caliente	Perrito kaaliente
Ice	Hielo(m)	Ielo
Ice cream	Helado(m)	Elaado
Ice-cube	Cubito(m)de hielo	Kubito de ielo
Indian tea	Té(m)indio	Té indio
Invert sugar	Azúcar(m)invertido	Athúkaar invertido
Jam	Mermelada(f)	Mermelaadaa
Jelly	Gelatina(f)	Khelaatina
Junk food	Comida(f)basura	Komida basura
Kebab	Kebab(m)	Kebaab

Lamb meat	Carne(f)de cordero	Karne de kordero
Lamb chop	Chuleta(f)de cordero	Chooleta de-kordero
Lemon cheese	Cuajado(m)de limón	Kuakhado de limón
Lentil soup	Sopa(f)de lentejas	Sopaa de-lentekhaas
Lima bean	Judía(f)de la peladilla	Khudía de la-peladilla
Lunch	Almuerzo(m)	Aalmuertho
Luncheon meat	Carne(f)en conserva	Karne en-konservaa
Macaroni	Macarrones(mpl)	Makarrones
Main course	Plato(m) principal	Plaato printhipaal
Margarine	Margarina(f)	Maargaarina
Mayonnaise	Mayonesa(f)	Mayonesa
Meal	Komida(f)	Komida
Meat	Carne(f)	Kaarne
Meat pie	Pastel(m)de carne	Paastel de karne
Meatless diet	Dieta(f)sicarne	Dieta sin karne
Mincemeat	Carne(f)picada	Karne pikaada
Mutton	Karne(f) de cordero	Karne de kordero
Noodles	Fideos(mpl)	Fideos
Noodle soup	Sopa(f)de fideos	Sopaa de fideos
Nougat	Turrón(m)	Turrón
Oatmeal	Harina(f)de avena	Arina de avena
Oil	Aceite(m)	Athiete
Olive oil	Aceite(m)de oliva	Athelte de oliva
Omelette	Tortilla(f)	Tortilla
Pasta	Pasta(f)	Paasta
Pastries	Pastas(fpl)	Paastas

Peanut butter	Manteca(f)de cacahuete	Manteka de-kakauete
Peanut oil	Aceite de cacahuete	Atheite de-kakauete
Pea soup	Sopa(f)de guisantes	Sopa de-gisaantes
Pepperoni	Pepperoni(m)	Pepperoni
Pickle	Encurtido(m)	Enkurtido
Pickled onions	Cebollas(fpl)en vinagre	Thebollas en-vinaagre
Pie(of fruit)	Pastel(m)	Paastel
Pie(of meat)	Empanada(f)	Empaanaada
Piecrust	Pasta(f)de pastel	Paasta de paastel
Pizza	Pizza(f)	Pizza
Pork	Karne de cerdo(f)	Karne de therdo
Pork sausage	Salchicha(f)de cerdo	Saalchicha de-therdo
Potato cake	Croqueta(f)de patata	Krokete de-paatata
Pulse	Legumbre(f)	Legoombre
Rice	Arroz(m)	Arroth
Rice pudding	Arroz(m)con leche	Arroth kon leche
Roast	Carne(f)asada	Kaarne asada
Roast beef	Rosbif(m)	Rosbif
Salad	Ensalada(f)	Ensalaada
Salad-cream	Mayonesa(f)	Mayonesa
Salad-dressing	Mayonesa(f)	Mayonesa
Salad-oil	Aceite(m)para ensaladas	Atheite para-ensalaadas
Salmon	Salmón(m)	Salmón

Salt	Sal(f)	Saal
Salt beef	Carne(f)de vaca salada	Karne de vaka-salaada
Sandwich	Sándwich(m)	Sándwich
Sardine	Sardina(f)	Saardina
Sauce	Salsa(f)	Salsaa
Sausage	Embutido(m)	Embutido
Sausage(small)	Salchicha(f)	Saalchicha
Sausage-meat	Carne(f)de salchicha	Karne de-salchicha
Sausage-roll	Empanadilla(f)de-salchicha	Empanadilla de-salchicha
Seafood	Mariscos(mpl)	Mariskos
Sesame oil	Aceite(m)de sésaamo	Atheite de-sésaamo
Shrimp sauce	Salsa(f)de camarones	Saalsa de-kamarones
Snack	Bocadillo(m)	Bokadillo
Soft ice cream	Helado(m)de máquina	Elaado de mákina
Soup(thick)	Sopa(f)	Sopa
Soup(clear)	Caldo(m)	Kaaldo
Sour cream	Nata(f)cortada	Naata kortaada
Sourdough bread	Pan(m)de masa-fermentada	Paan de masa-fermentaada
Soya	Sokha(f)	Sokha
Soya flour	Harina(f)de soja	Arina de sokha
Soya oil	Aceite(m)de soja	Atheite de sokha
Soya sauce	Salsa de soja(f)	Salsaa de sokha
Spaghetti	Espaguetis(mpl)	Espaagaytis
Sprout	Brote(m)	Brote
Stock	Caldo(m)	Kaaldo

Sugar	Azúcar(m)	Azúkar
Sugar cube	Terrón(m)de azúcar	Terrón de-athúkaar
Sugar candy	Azúkar(m)candi	Athúkar kandi
Sugar free	Sin azúcar(m)	Athúkaar
Sugar loaf	Pan(m)de azúkar	Paan de athúkaar
Sweetener	Edulcorante(m)	Edukoraante
Sweetmeats	Dulces(mpl)	Doolthes
Sweets	Dulces(mpl)	Doolthes
Syrup	Jarabe(m)	Kharaabe
Tartar sauce	Salsa(f)tártara	Saalsa tártaara
Teacake	Bollito(m)	Bollito
Toast	Pan(m)tostado	Paan tostaado
Toasted sandwich	Såndwich(m) tostado	Sándwich-tostaado
Tomato ketchup	Salsa(f)de tomate	Salsaa de tomaate
Tomato puree	Puré(m)de tomate	Puré de tomate
Tomato sauce	Salsa(f)de tomate	Salsa de tomaate
Vegetable fat	Grasa(f)vegetal	Graasa vekhetaal
Vegetable oil	Aceite(m)vegetal	Atheite vekhetaal
Vegetable salad	Ensalada(f)verde	Ensalaada verde
Vegetable soup	Sopa(f)de hortelano	Sopa de ortelaano
Venison	Carne(f)de venado	Karne de venado
Vinegar	Vinagre(m)	Vinagre
Wafer(biscuit)	Galleta(f)	Galleta
Wafer(icecream)	Barquillo(m)	Barkillo
Wheatmeal	Harina(f)de trigo	Arina de trigo
White bread	Pan(m)blanco	Paan blaanko
White meat	Carne(f)blanca	Karne blaanka
Whole food	Comida(f)naturista	Komida-naatoorista

Wholemeal bread	Pan(m)integral	Paan integraal
Wholemeal flour	Harina(f)integral	Arina integraal

*churros-popular spanish snack.They are long fritters made with flour and water.often eaten with hot choclate as a breakfast.In Madrid,a thicker variety called porra is more popular.

*paella-poular spanish dish.Is something similar to indian biryani.

A piece of bread	Un pedazo de pan	Un pedatho de-paan
A piece of cake	Una porción de tarta	Una porthión de-taarta
A pinch of	Un\a pizca de	Un\a pithka de
A dash of	Poquito de	Pokito de
A handful of	Puñado de	Puniado de
A slice	Una loncha	Oona loncha
Bite size	Cortado a toquitos	Kortaado a-tokitos
Bittersweet	Agridulce	Agridoolthe
Calories	Caloría(f)	Kaloría
Canned foods	Conservas(fpl)-alimenticias	Konservas-aalimentithias
Cooked	Cocido/a	Kothido/a
Cuisine	Cocina(f)	Kothina
Deep frozen	Ultracongelado	Ultrakonkhelaado
Deep fry	Freír(v)en aceite-abundante	Freír en atheite-abundaante
Diet	Dieta(f)	Dieta
Dried	Seco/a	Seko/a
Fried	Frito	Frito
Fresh	Fresco/a	Fresko/a
Fried egg	Huevo(m)frito	Ooevo frito

Frozen	Congelado	Konkhelaado
Genetically modified	Transgénico	Transkhéniko
Gluten-free	Sin gluten	Sin glooten
Grilled	Asado a la parilla	Asado a la parilla
Hard boiled egg	Huevo(m)cocido	Ooevo kothido
Helping	Porción(f)	Porthión
I am full	No puedo más	No puedo máas
Low-fat	Bajo en grasas	Bakho en grasas
Low in sugar	Bajo en azúcar	Bakho en athúkar
Nutrient	Nutriente(m)	Nutriente
Nutritious	Nutritivo	Nutritivo
Oily	Grasiento	Grasiento
Organic	Orgánico	Orgániko
Preservative	Preservativo(m)	Preservativo
Preserved food	En conserva	En konserva
Poultry	Aves	Aves
Raw	Crudo/a	Krudo/a
Readt to serve	Preparado	Preparado
Refreshing	Refrescante	Refreskaante
Refrigerate	Refrigerar(v)	Refrikheraar
Roasted	Asado\a	Asaado\a
Salt-free	Sin sal	Sin saal
Sauté	Salteado	Saalteado
Scrambled egg	Huevo(m)resuelto	Ooevo resooelto
Season	Sazonado\a	Sathonaado\a
Season	Sazonar(v)	Sathonaar
Seasoning	Condimento(m)	Kondimento
Slice(meat)	Tajada(f)	Takhaada
Slice(sausage)	Raja(f)	Rakha
Slice(bread)	Rebanada(f)	Rebanaada
Slice(lemon)	Rodaja(f)	Rodaakha

Smoked	Ahumado\a	Aumaado\a
Soft boiled egg	Huevo(m)pasado-por agua	Ooevo pasado-por aagooa
Sour	Agrio\a	Agrio\a
Special dish	Plato(m)del día	Plaato del día
Spicy	Picante	Pikaante
Sprinkle	Rociada(f)	Rothiada
Squeeze of lemon	Unas goats de limón	Unas gotaas de-limón
Stir fry	Sofrito(m)	Sofrito
Tangy	Fuerte y picante	Fooerte y pikaante
Tempting	Apetitoso	Apetitoso

I am on a special diet.
Estoy a régimen especial.
Estoy a rékhimen espethial.

I am a vegetarian.
Soy vegetariano/a.
Soy vekhetariano/a.

Is it sweet enough for you?
¿Te he puesto bastante azúcar?
¿Te e pooesto baastante athúkar?

It's very salted.
Está muy salado.
Está muy salaado.

I am allergic to dairy products.
Soy alérgico/a a los productos lácteos.
Soy alérkhiko a los prodooktos lákteos.

This recipe serves 4.
Esta receta es suficiente para 4 personas.
Esta retheta es soofithiente para 4 personaas.

Note-Tener is a commonly used verb to describe a personal condition where english uses be+an adjective.
E.g.1.to be hungry-tener hambre

I am hungry.
Tengo hambre.
Tengo aambre.

I am famished.
Tengo un hambre canina.
Tengo un aambre kanina.

We are hungry.
Tenemos hambre
Tenemos aambre.

2. to be thirsty-tener sed
We were thirsty.
Teníamos sed.
Teníamos sed.

Chapter 2

Beverages
Bebidas

English	Spanish	Pronunciation
After-dinner drink	Copa(f) después-de la cena	Kopa después-de la thena
Apple juice	Zumo(m)de manzana	Thumo de-manthana
Beer	Cerveza(f)	Thervetha
Black coffee	Café(m)solo	Kafé solo
Bottle of beer(250ml)	Botellín(m)	Botellín
Bottled beer	Cerveza(f)de botella	Thervetha de-botella
Bottled water	Agua(f)embotellada	Aagooa-embotellada
Brandy	Brandy(m)	Braandy
Buttermilk	Suero(m)de leche	Suero de leche
Cappucino	Capuchino(m)	Kapuchino
Champagne	Champaña(f)	Champania
Club soda	Agua(f)de sifón	Aagooa de sifón
Cocktail	Kombinado(m)	Kombinado
Coffee whitener	Leche(f)en polvo	Leche en polvo
Cognac	Coñac(m)	Coniak
Dark beer	Cerveza(f)negra	Thervetha negra
Decaffeinated	Descafeinado	Deskafeinaado
Dessert wine	Vino(m)dulce	Vino doolthe
Draught beer	Cerveza(f)de barril	Thervetha de-barril

Drinking choclate	Chocolate(m)bebida	Chokolate bebida
Coffee with milk	Café(m)con leche	Kafé kon leche
Espresso cof-	Café(m)exprés	Kafé exprés
Fruit cocktail	Cóctel(m)de frutas	Kóktel de-frootaas
Fruit juice	Zumo(m)de frutas	Thumo de-frootaas
Gin	Ginebra(f)	Khinebra
Ginger beer	Gaseosa(f)de jenjibre	Gaseosa de-khenkhibre
Ice cold	Helado	Elaado
Ice cream soda	Soda(f)mezclada-con helados	Soda methklada-kon elado
Iced water	Agua helada	Agooa elaada
Juice	Zumo(m)	Thumo
Lemonade	Limonada(f)	Limonada
Lemon juice	Zumo(m)de limón	Thumo de limón
Lemon squash	Bebida(f)de limón	Bebida de limón
Lemon tea	Té(m)con limón	Té kon limón
Light beer	Cerveza(f)rubia	Thervetha roobia
Liquor	Bebidas(fpl)fuertes	Bebidas fooertes
Litre bottle of beer	Litrona(f)	Litrona
Malt liquor	Cerveza(f)	Thervetha
Malt whisky	Whisky(m)de malta	Whisky de maalta
Malting barley	Cebada(f)cervecera	Thebaada-thervethera
Bottle of beer(300ml)	Mediana	Mediana
Milk choclate	Chocolate(m)con leche	Chokolaate kon-leche
Milkshake	Batido(m)con leche	Baatido kon leche
Mineral water	Agua(f)mineral	Agooa mineral

Neat gin	Ginebra(f)pura	Khinebra poora
Nonalcoholic beer	Cerveza(f)sin alcohol	Thervetha sin-alkool
Orangeade	Naranjada(f)	Naarankhada
Orange juice	Zumo(m)de naranja	Thumo de-naarankha
Red wine	Vino(m)tinto	Vino tinto
Rum	Ron(m)	Ron
Sangría-(red wine punch)	Sangría(f)	Sangría
Semi skimmed milk	Leche(f)semidesnatada	Leche-semidesnatada
Sherry	Jerez(m)	Khereth
Skimmed milk	Leche(f)desnatada	Leche desnatada
Soft drink	Bebida(f)refrescante	Bebida-refreskante
Spirits	Licores(mpl)	Likores
Tea	Té(m)	Té
Tequila	Tequila(m)	Tekila
Vodka	Vodka(m)	Vodka
Whisky	Whisky	Whisky
White coffee	Café(m) con leche	Kafé kon leche
White wine	Vino(m) blanco	Vino blanko
Wine	Vino(m)	Vino

A bottle/glass of red wine
Una botella/copa de vino tinto.
Oona botella/kopa de vino tinto.

A bottle/glass of rose wine.
Una botella/copa de vino rosado.
Oona botella/copa de vino rosado.

A pint of beer.
Una pinta de cerveza.
Oona pinta de thervetha.

A shot of gin/rum.
Un chupito de ginebra/ron.
Oon chupito de khinebra/ron.

A shot of tequila/vodka/whisky.
Un chupito de tequila/vodka/güisqui.
Oon chupito de tekila/vodka/gweeskee.

A glass of beer.
Una caña de cerveza.
Ona cania de thervetha.

A bottle/glass of sparkling wine.
Una botella/copa de vinoespumoso.
Oona botella/kopa de vino espoomoso.

A jug of beer.
Una jarra de cerveza.
Oona kharra de thervetha.

A bottle/glass of white wine.
Una botella/copa de vino blanco.
Oona botella/kopa de vino blanko.

Chapter 3

Vegetables
Legumbres

English	Spanish	Pronunciation
Aubergine	Berenjena (f)	Berenkhena
Beans	Judías(fpl)	Khudeeas
Beetroot	Romolacha(f)	Romolacha
Cabbage	Col(f)	kol
Carrot	Zanahoria(f)	Thanaoria
Cauliflower	Coliflor(f)	Koliflor
Coriander	Culantro(m)	Kulantro
Cucumber	Pepino(m)	Pepino
French bean	Judía(f)enana	Khudeea enana
Garlic	Ajo(m)	Akho
Ginger	Jengibre(m)	Khenkhibre
Lemon	Limón(m)	Limón
Lettuce	Lechuga(f)	Lechuga
Mint	Menta(f)	Menta
Onion	Cebolla(f)	Thebolla
Peas	Guisantes(mpl)	Guisantes
Pepper	Pimiento(m)	Pimiento
Potato	Patata(f)	Patata
Radish	Rabano(m)	Rabano
Soyabean	Haba(f)de soja	Aba de sokha
Spinach	Espinacas	Espinakas
Sweetpea	Guisante(m)de olor	Guisante de olor
Tomato	Tomate(m)	Tomate
Turnip	Nabo(m)	Nabo

Chapter 4

Fruits
Frutas

English	Spanish	Pronunciation
Almond	Almendra(f)	Almendra
Apple	Manzana(f)	Manthana
Apricot	Albaricoque(m)	Albarikoke
Banana	Plátano(m)	Plátaano
Blackberry	Zarzamora(f)	Zarzamora
Cherry	Cereza(f)	Theretha
Chestnut	Castaña	Kastania
Citrusfruits	Agrios(mpl)	Agrios
Coconut	Coco(m)	Koko
Crabapple	Manzana(f)silvestre	Manthana-silvestre
Currant	Pasa(f) de Korinto	Pasa de Korinto
Custardapple	Chirimoya(f)	Chirimoya
Date	Dátil(m)	Dátil
Fig	Higo(m)	Igo
Grapefruit	Toronja(f)	Toronkha
Guava	Guayaba(f)	Guayaba
Groundnut	Cacahuete(m)	Kakauete
Mango	Mango(m)	Mango
Orange	Naranja(f)	Narankha
Papaya	Papaya(f)	Papaya
Pear	Pera(f)	Pera
Pineapple	Ananás	Ananás
Pistachio	Pistacho(m)	Pistacho
Pomegranate	Granada(f)	Granada

Prune	Ciruela(F)pasa	Thiruela pasa
Raisin	Pasa(f)	Pasa
Sugarcane	Caña(f)de azúcar	Kania de athúkar
Sweetpotato	Batata(f)	Batata
Tamarind	Tamarindo(m)	Tamarindo
Watermelon	Sandía(f)	Sandía

Chapter 5

Spices
Especias

English	Spanish	Pronunciation
Alum	Alumbre(m)	Aloombre
Aniseed	Anís(m)	Anees
Bayleaf	Hoja(f)de laurel	Okha de laurel
Blackpepper	Pimienta(m)	Pimienta
Camphor	Alcanfor(m)	Alkanfor
Cardamom	Cardamomo(m)	Kardamomo
Chilli	Ají(m)	Akhí
Chilli powder	Polvos(mpl)de chile	Polvos de chile
Cinnamon	Canela(f)	Kanela
Clove	Clavo de especia	Klavo de espethia
Cuminseed	Comino(m)	Komino
Greenpepper	Pimienta(f)verde	Pimienta verde
Mace	Macis(f)	Mathis
Mint	Menta(f)	Menta
Musk	Almizcleña(f)	Almithklenia
Mustard	Mostaza(f)	Mostatha
Nutmeg	Nuez(f)moscada	Nueth moskada
Oregano	Orégano(m)	Orégaano
Parsley	Perejil(m)	Perekhil
Saffron	Azafrán(m)	Athafrán
Turmeric	Cúrcuma(f)	Kúrkuma
Whitepepper	Pimienta(f)blanca	Pimienta blanka

Chapter 6

Ailments
Enfermedades

English	Spanish	Pronunciation
Accident	accidente(m)	akthidente
Acidity	acedía(f)	athedía
Acne	acné(f)	akné
AIDS	SIDA	SIDA
Aids test	test(m)de SIDA	test **de** SIDA
Ailments	enfermedades(fpl)	enfermedades
Allergy	alergia(F)	alerkhia
Ambulance	ambulancia(f)	ambulancia
Anaesthetic	anestesia(f)	anestesia
Antibiotics	antibióticos	antibiótikos
Antihistamines	antihistamínicos(mpl)	antiistamínikos
Anti inflammatories	anti inflamatorios	anti inflamaatorios
Appendicitis	apendicitis(f)	apendithitis
Aspirin	aspirina(f)	aspirina
Asthma	asma(f)	asma
Baldness	calvicie(f)	kalvithie
Bandage	venda(f)	venda
Belching	eructar	eruktar
Bile	bilis(f)	bilis
Bleeding	sangrante	sangraante
Blindness	ceguedad(f)	cegeHad
Blister	ampolla(f)	ampolla
Blood	sangre(f)	saangre
Blood flow	flujo(m)sanguíneo	flukho sanguíneo

Blood group	grupo(m)sanguíneo	grupo sanguíneo
Bloodpoisoning	envenenamiento(m)de la sangre	envenenamiento de la sangre
Blood pressure	presión(f)sanguínea	presión-sanguínea
Breath	aliento(m)	aliento
Bronchitis	bronquitis(f)	bronchitis
Bruise	contusion(f)	kontusión
Burn	quemadura(f)	kemadura
Cardiacarrest	paro(m)cardíaco	paro kardíako
Cataract	catarata(f)	katarata
Casualty	urgencias	oorkhenthias
Chemotherapy	quimioterapia(f)	kimioterapia
Chickenpox	varicela(f)	varithela
Chilblain	sabañón(m)	sabanión
Chill	escalofrío(m)	eskalofrío
Cholera	cólera(m)	kólera
Clinic	clínica(f)	klínika
Colic	cólico(m)	kóliko
Concussion	conmoción(f)cerebral	konmothión-therebraal
Condom	condón(m)	kondón
Conjunctivitis	conjuntivitis(f)	konkhuntivitis
Constipation	estreñimiento(m)	estrenimiento
Consumption	tisis(f)	tisis
Contact lenses	lentes de contacto	lentes de-kontakto
Contagious	contagioso	kontakhioso
Contraceptive	contraceptivo	kontraceptivo
Cough	tos(f)	tos
Cramp	calambre(m)	kalambre

Cure	cura(f)	kura
Cystitis	cistitis(f)	thistitis
Depressed	deprimido/a	deprimido/a
Dermatologist	dermatólogo(m)	dermatólogo
Diabetes	diabetes(f)	diabetes
Diagnosis	diagnóstico	diagnóstiko
Diarrhoea	diarrea(f)	diarrea
Disease	enfermedad(f)	enfermedad
Dispensary	dispensario(m)	dispensario
Dizziness	vertigo(m)	vértigo
Dizzy	mareado/a	mareado/a
Doctor	médico(m)	médiko
Dose	dosis(f)	dosis
Drugstore	farmacia(f)	farmacia
Dumbness	mudez(f)	mudez
Dwarf	enano(m)	enano
Dysentry	disentería(f)	disentería
Eczema	eczema(m)	ekthema
ENT	otorrinolaringología(f)	otorrinlarin-golokhía
Epidemic	epidemia(f)	epidemia
Epilepsy	epilepsia(f)	epilepsia
Faint	desmayo(m)	desmaayo
Fever	fiebre(f)	fiebre
Filling	empaste(m)	empaaste
First aid	asistencia sanitaria	asistenthia-sanitaria
Fistula	fistula(f)	fístula
Flu	gripe(f)	gripe
Food poisoning	botulismo(m)	botulismo

Fungal	micótico	mikótiko
Gall-bladder	vesícula(f)biliar	vesíkula biliaar
Giddiness	vértigo(m)	vértigo
Gland	glándula(f)	glándula
Glasses	gafas	gaafas
Gonorrhoea	gonorrea(f)	gonorrea
Griping	retortijante	retortikhante
Gynaecologist	ginecólogo(m)	khinekólogo
Have cold	estar(v)resfriado	estar resfriado
Headache	dolor(m)de cabeza	dolor de kabetha
Heart	corazón(m)	korathón
Heart-attack	ataque(m)cardíaco	atake kardíako
Hernia	hernia(f)	ernia
Hiccup	hipo(m)	ipo
High blood pressure	hipertensión(f)	ipertensión
HIV negative	VIH negativo	VIH negaativo
HIV positive	VIH positivo	VIH poositivo
Homoeopathy	homeopatía(f)	omeopatía
Hospital	hospital(m)	ospitaal
Hunger	hambre(f)	ambre
Indigestion	indigestión(f)	indikhesteeón
Infection	infección(f)	infekthión
Inflammation	inflamación(f)	inflamathión
Inhaler	inhalador(m)	inhalaador
Injection	inyección(f)	inyekthión
Injury	herida(f)	erida
Insomnia	insomnio(m)	insomnio
Itch	picazón(f)	pikathón
Jaundice	ictericia(f)	ikterícia
Kidneystone	cálculo(m)renal	kálkulo renaal
Leprosy	lepra(f)	lepra

Leukaemia	leucemia(f)	leuthemia
Madness	demencia(f)	dementhia
Measles	sarampión(m)	sarampión
Medicine	medicina(f)	medithina
Menstruation	menstruación(f)	menstruathión
Migraine	jaqueca(f)	khakeka
Mumps	paperas(fpl)	paperaas
Nausea	bascas(fpl)	baskas
Nosebleed	hemorragia(f)nasal	emorrakhia nasal
Operate	opcrar(v)	opcraar
Pain	dolor(m)	dolor
Paediatrician	pediatra(m,f)	pediatra
Paralysis	parálisis(f)	paralysis
Penicillin	penicilina	penithilina
Pharmacy	farmacía	farmathía
Phlegm	flema(f)	flema
Piles	almorranas(fpl)	almorranas
Plaster	escayola(f)	eskayola
Plug	tampón(m)	tampón
Pneumonia	pulmonía(f)	pulmonía
Pregnant	embarazada	embarathada
Prescription	receta(f)	retheta
Pull muscle	torcerse(v)	tortherse
Pulse	latido(m)	latido
Pus	pus(m)	pus
Rheumatism	reumatismo(m)	reumatismo
Ringworm	tiña(f)	tinia
Roundworm	lombriz(f)intestinal	lombrith intestinal
Saliva	saliva(f)	saliva
Sanitary napkin	paño(m)higiénico	panio higiéniko

Sex perversity	perversidad(f)sexual	perservidaad sexooal
Shiver	temblor(m)	temblor
Shivery	destemplado/a	destemplado/a
Shock	shock	shock
Short sightedness	miopía(f)	meopeea
Sick	enfermo	enfermo
Side effect	efecto(m)secundario	efecto secundario
Sinusitis	sinusitis(f)	synusytis
Sleeping pill	somnífero	somnífero
Sneeze	estornudo(m)	estornudo
Sore throat	dolor(m)de garganta	dolor de-gargaanta
Sprain	torcedura(f)	torthedura
Sting	punzada(f)	punthada
Stomachache	dolor(m)de estómago	dolor de-estómago
Stool	cámaras(fpl)	kámaras
Sunburn	bronceado(m)	brontheado
Sunstroke	insolación(f)	insolación
Surgery	cirugía(f)	cirukhía
Sweat	sudor(m)	sudor
Swelling	tumefacción(f)	tumefakción
Syringe	jeringa(f)	kheringa
Tablet	tableta(f)	tableta
Tetanus	tétanos(m)	tétanos
Thermometer	termómetro(m)	termómetro
Treatment	tratamiento(m)	tratamiento
Tumour	tumor(m)	tumor
Typhus	tifus(m)	teefus

Urine	orina(f)	oreena
Vaccination	vacunación(f)	vakunación
Visiting hours	horas de visita	oras de visita
Vomiting	vómito(m)	vómito
Ward	sala(f)	saala
Weak	débil	débil
Wheelchair	silla(f)dc ruedas	silla de ruedas
Wound	herida(f)	erida
X-ray	radiografía(f)	radiografía

Where is the pharmacy/clinic?
¿Dónde está la farmacia?
¿Dónde está la farmathia?

Is there a night chemist nearby?
¿Hay una farmacia de guardía por aquí?
¿Ay oona farmathia de gooardía por akí?

Is there a chemist nearby?
¿Hay una farmacia de guardía aquí?
¿Ay oona farmathia de gooardía aquí?

Where is the nearest hospital?
¿Dónde está el hospital más cercano?
¿Dónde está l ospitaal más therkano?

Where is the Casualty?
¿Dónde está las urgencias?
¿Dónde está las oorkhenthias?

What are the visiting hours?
¿Cuáles son las horas de visita?
¿Kuáles son las oras de visita?

Where is ward no.6?
¿Dónde está la planta núm.seis?
¿Dónde está la planta núm.seis?

I need this medicine, please.
Necesito esta medicina, por favor.
Nethesiti esta medithina, por favor.

Please give me medicine to cure. . .
Déme una medicina para curar. . .
Déme una medithina para kuraar.

Is it available only on prescription?
¿Está obtenible sólo con receta?
¿Está obtenible sólo kon retheta?

I have the precription.
Tengo receta médica.
Tengo retheta médika.

What do you prescribe?
¿Qué me recomienda?
¿Ké me rekomienda?

How many times a day?
¿Cuántas veces al día?
¿Kuántas vethes al día?

Twice a day.
Dos veces al día.
Dos vethes al día.

Have you taken this before?
¿Ha tomado esto antes?
¿A tomaado esto antes?

It is made according to prescription.
Está hecha según receta.
Está echa según retheta.

Can you order this medicine for me?
¿Podría hacer un pedido de este medicina?
¿Podría ather un pedido de esta medithina?

When can I pick it up?
¿Cuándo podría recogerla?
¿Kuándo podría rekokherla?

It will be ready to pick up in 15 minutes.
Estará listo en quince minutos.
Estará listo en kinthe minootos.

I feel sick.
Estoy mareado(m)/mareada(f).
Estoy mareado(m)/mareada

I suffer from boils.
Tengo diviesos.
Tengo diviesos.

I feel ill.
Me siento mal.
Me siento maal.

I suffer from rheumatism.
Padezco de reumatismo.
Padethko de reumaatismo.

You can buy it over the counter.
Esto se compra sin receta obligatoria.
Esta se kompra sin retheta obligaatoria.

Please get the doctor.
Por favor llame al medico.
Por favor llame al medico.

Quickly!Help!Medical care!
¡Pronto!¡Socorro!¡Atención médica!
¡Pronto!¡Sokorro!¡Atenthión médika!

Can I see a female doctor?
¿Puede examinarme una doctora?
¿Pooede examinarme oona doktora?

I can't help coughing.
No puedo dejar de toser.
No puedo dekhar de toser.

Are you on medication?
¿Se encuentra bajo medicación?
¿Se enkuentra bakho medikathión?

I am on regular medication for. . .
Estoy bajo medicaciónpara. . .
Estoy bakho medikathión para. .

It would be helpful if you could come and see the patient.
Sería bueno que pudiera venir y examinar el enfermo /la enferma.
Sería bueno ke pudiera venir y examinar l enfermo/la enferma.

Which doctor is treating you?
¿Qué médico le atiende?
¿Ké médico le atiende?

I cannot tolerate the heat.
No puedo aguantar el calor.
No puedo agooantaar l kalor.

The doctor prescribed complete rest.
El médico recomendó el reposo completo.
L médico rekomendó l reposo kompleto.

I will prescribe you a preventive medicine.
Le recetará una medicina preventiva.
Le rethetará una medithina preventiva.

He hurt his hand.
Se lastimó la mano.
Se lastimó la mano.

I have a toothache.
Me duele una muela.
Me dooele oona mooela.

Where does it hurt you?
¿Dónde le duele?
¿Dónde le duele?

My head aches.
Me duele la cabeza.
Me duela la kabetha.

I don't have an appetite.
No tengo apetito.
No tengo apetito.

My stomach aches.
Me duele el estómago.
Me duele l estómaago.

Does it hurt much?
¿Duele mucho?
¿Duele mucho?

How do you feel?
¿Qué tal le encuentra?
¿Ké taal le enkuentra?

I am constipated.
Estoy estreñido/estreñida.
Estoy estrniedo/estrenieda.

I am dehydrated.
Estoy deshidratado.
Estoy desidrataado.

I fell down the stairs.
Caí rodando por la escalera.
Caí rodando por la eskalera.

That made me sick.
Eso me dio ganas de vomitar.
Eso me dio gaanas de vomitaar.

Do you take take drugs?
¿Toma drogas?
¿Toma drogas?

Can I see someone who practices naturopathy?
¿Puedo ver a alguien que practique naturopatía?
¿Pooedo ver a aalgien ke praktike naaturopatía?

I am on the pill.
Tomo la píldora.
Tomo la píldora.

I have been injured.
He sido herido/a.
E sido erido/a.

I have a history of. . .
Hay antecedentes de. . .
Ay antethedentes de. . .

You need to be admitted to hospital.
Necesita ingresar en un hospital.
Nethesita ingresaar en oon ospitaal.

He needs a blood transfusion.
Él necesita una transfusión de sangre.
I. nethesita oona transfoosión de saangre.

What is your blood group?
¿Qué es su grupo sanguíneo?
¿Ké es su groopo sangíneo?

Can you donate blood?
¿Puede donar sangre?
¿Pooedes donaar saangre?

Please use a new syringe.
Por favor use una jeringa nueva.
Por favor oose oona kheringa nooeva.

I think I am pregnant.
Creo que estoy embarazada.
Kreo ke estoy embarathada.

Are you using contraception?
¿Usa anticonceptivos?
¿Oosa antikontheptivos?

Part-VI
Chapter 1

Travel

Around The Town
Por La Ciudad

English	Spanish	Pronunciation
Airport	Aeropuerto(m)	Aeropooerto
Amusement park	Parque(m)de atracciones	Parke de-atrakthiones
Antique shop	Tienda(f)de-antiguedades	Tienda de-antiguedades
A one day excursion	Un billete de ida y vuelta	Un billete de ida y Vuelta
Area	Región(f)	Rekhión
Bakery	Panadería(f)	Panadería
Bar	Bar(m)	Bar
Barber shop	Barbería(f)	Barbería
Bazaar	Bazar(m)	Bathar
Beach	Playa(f)	Playa
Beauty parlour	Salón(m)de belleza	Salón de belletha
Bicycle	Bicicleta(f)	Bithikleta
Boarding house	Pensión(f)	Pensión
Boating holiday	Vacaciones(fpl)en barca	Vakathiones en-barka
Boating trip	Paseo(m)en barca	Paseo en barka
Boat-train	Tren(m)del barco	Tren del barko

Bookshop	Librería(f)	Librería
Border	Frontera(f)	Frontera
Botanical garden	Jardín(m)botánico	Khardín botániko
Bridge	Puente(m)	Pooente
Building	Edificio(m)	Edifithio
Bus	Autobús(m)	Autobús
Butcher's shop	Carnecería(f)	Karnethería
Café	Kafé	Kafé
Camping ground	Terreno de cámping	Terreno de-kámping
Candy store	Confitería(f)	Konfitería
Capital city	Capital(f)	Kapitaal
Carpentry	Carpintería(f)	Karpintería
Cart	Carro(m)	Karro
Casino	Casino(m)	Kasino
Castle	Castillo	Kastillo
Cathedral	Catedral(f)	Katedraal.
Cathedral church	Iglesia(f)catedral	Iglesia katedraal
Cave	Cueva(f)	Kooeva
Chemist's shop	Farmacia(f)	Farmathia
Chinatown	Barrio(m)chino	Barrio chino
Church	Iglesia(f)	Iglesia
Club	Club(m)	Kloob
Cinema	Cine(m)	Thine
Cinema complex	Cine(m)multisalas	Thine mooltisaalas
Circus	Circo(m)	Thirko
City	Ciudad(f)	Thiudaad
City center	Centro(m)de la ciudad	Thentro de la-thiudad
Cityscape	Paisaje(m)urbana	Paisakhe oorbaana
Coffee shop	Café(m)	Kafé

Concert	Concierto(m)	Konthierto
Consulate	Consulado(m)	Konsulaado
Corner shop	Tienda(f)de esquina	Tienda de eskina
Cornet	Cucurucho(m)	Kukuroocho
Countryclub	Club(m)campestre	Klub kampestre
Countrycottage	Casita(f)en el campo	Kasita en l kampo
Country road	Camino(m)vecinal	Kamino vethinaal
Countryside	Campo(m)	Kaampo
Court(law)	Tribunal(m)	Tribunaal
Crossing(road)	Paso(m)para peatones	Paso para-peatones
Crowd	Multitud(f)	Mooltitud
Dairyfarm	Granja(f)	Grankha
Dead end	Callejón(m)sin salida	Kallekhón sin-saalida
Department store	Almacenes(mpl)	Almathenes
Discothèque	Discoteca(f)	Diskoteka
District	Barrio(m)	Barrio
Ditch(road)	Cuneta(f)	Kooneta
Drive in cinema	Autocine(m)	Aootothine
Drugstore	Farmacia(f)	Farmathia
Drycleaner's	Tintorería(f)	Tintorería
Electricidad	Electricidad(f)	Elektrithidaad
Embassy	Embajada(f)	Embakhaada
Excursion	Excursión(f)	Exkursión
Excursion train	Tren(m)de excursión	Tren de excursión
Exhibition	Exposición(f)	Exposithión
Factory	Fábrica(f)	Fábrika
Farm	Granja(f)	Graankha
Farmhouse	Cortijo(m)	Kortikho

Fence	Cerca(f)	Therka
Field	Prado(m)	Praado
Fire-department	Cuerpo(m)de bomberas	Kuerpo de bomberaas
Fishing	Pesca(f)	Peska
Fish market	Pescadería(f)	Peskadería
Flea market	Mercado(m)de barajitas y cosas usadas	Mcrkado de-barakhitas y kosaas oosaadas
Flower shop	Florería(f)	Florería
Flower-show	Exposición(f)de flores	Exposithión de-flores
Fort	Fortín(m)	Fortín
Fortress	Fortaleza(f)	Fortaletha
Fountain	Fuente(f)	Fooente
Fruit shop	Frutería(f)	Frootería
Furniture shop	Tienda(f)de muebles	Tienda de-mooebles
Gallery(art)	Museo(m)	Mooseo
Garden	Jardín(m)	Khardín
Gate	Puerta(f)	Pooerta
Golf-course	Campo(m)de golf	Kampo de golf
Granary	Granero(m)	Granero
Grave	Sepultura(f)	Sepooltoora
Greengrocer's shop	Verdulería	Verdulería
Grocer's shop	Tienda(f)de ultramarines	Tienda de-Ooltramarines
Guesthouse	Pensión(f)	Pensión
Gutter	Arroyo(m)	Arroyo
Harbour	Puerto(m)	Pooerto
Hardware shop	Ferretería(f)	Ferretería

Hat shop	Sombrerería(f)	Sombrerería
Highrise building	Edificio(m)elevado	Edifithio elevaado
Highway	carretera(f)	karretera
Hill	Colina(f)	Kolina
Hospital	Hospital(m)	Ospitaal
Hotel	Hótel(m)	Ótel
House	Casa(f)	Kasa
Hut	Casilla(f)	Kasilla
Inn	Posada(f)	Posaada
Jewellery shop	Joyería(f)	Khoyería
Junk shop	Tienda(f)de trastos-viejos	Tienda de trastos-viekhos
Kindergarten	kindergarten(m)	kindergaarten
Lane	Callejón(m)	Kallekhón
Landscape	Paisaje(m)	Paisaakhe
Library	Biblioteca(f)	Biblioteka
Liquor store	Bodega(f)	Bodega
Lost and found	Oficina(f)de objetos-perdidos	Ofithina de-obkhetos perdidos
Lunatic asylum	Manicomio(m)	Manikomio
Market	Mercado(m)	Merkaado
Maternityhome	casa(f)de maternidad	kasa de-maaternidaad
Ministry	Ministerio(m)	Ministerio
Mosque	Mezquita(f)	Methkita
Motorcycle	Motocicleta(f)	Motothikleta
Mountain	Montaña(f)	Montania
Mountaineering	Montañismo(m)	Montaniesmo
Mountain range	Sierra(f)	Sierra
Museum	Museo(m)	Mooseo

Music-center	Equipo(m)estereofónico	Ekipo-estereofóniko
Music festival	Festival(m)de música	Festivaal de-músika
National park	Parque(m)nacional	Parke nathionaal
Nightclub	cabaret(m)	kabaret
Optician's shop	Óptica(f)	Óptika
Orphanage	Orfanato(m)	Orfanato
Park	Parque(m)	Parke
Pavilion	Pabellón(m)	Pabellón
Pawnshop	casa(f)de empeños	kasa de empenios
Place of amusement	Lugar(m)de diversion	Loogar de-diversion
Plants	Plantas(fpl)	Plantaas
Poultry shop	Pollería(f)	Pollería
Real estate	Bienes(mpl)raíces	Bienes raíthes
Restaurant	Restaurante(m)	Restaaooraante
Rickshaw	Jinrikisha(f)	Khinrikisha
River	Río(m)	Río
Road	Camino(m)	Kamino
Rural dispensary	Dispensario(m)rural	Dispensaario-rooral
School	Escuela(f)	Escooela
Scooter	Scooter(m)	Skooter
Sea food restaurant	Marisquería(f)	Mariskería
Second hand bookshop	Librería(f)	Librería
Second hand shop	Compraventa(f)	Kompraventa
Shoe shop	Zapatería(f)	Zapatería
Shop	Tienda(f)	Tienda
Shopping mall	Centro(m)commercial	Thentro-komerthial

Shopwindow	Escaparate(m)	Eskaparate
Snackbar	Cafetería(f)	Kafetería
Stadium	Estadio(m)	Estaadio
Station	Estación(f)	Estathión
Stationer's shop	Papelería(f)	Papelería
Street	calle(f)	kalle
Street lamp	farol(m)	faarol
Street market	mercado(m)callejero	merkado-kallekhero
Swimming pool	Piscina(f)	Pisthina
Tailor's shop	Sastrería(f)	Sastrería
Taxi	Taxi(m)	Taxi
Telephone booth	Cabina(f)de teléfono	Kabina de-teléfono
Temple	Templo(m)	Templo
Three wheeler	Coche(m)de tres ruedas	Koche de tres rooedas
Ticket	Entrada(f)	Entrada
Tomb	Tumba(f)	Toomba
Tower	Torre(f)	Torre
Town	Ciudad(f)	Thiudaad
Toy shop	Juguetería(f)	Khugaytería
Traffic	Tráfico(m)	Tráfiko
Traffic jam	Atasco(m)	Atasko
Traffic lights	Semáforo(m)	Semáforo
Traffic sign	Señal(m)de tráfico	Senial de tráfiko
Train	Tren(m)	Tren
Tram	Tranvía(f)	Tranvía
Travel agency	Agencia(f)de viajes	Akhenthia de-viakhes

Tree	Árbol(m)	Árbol
Truck	Carro(m)	Karro
University	Universidad(f)	Ooniversidaad
Valley	Valle(m)	Valle
Village(small)	Aldea(f)	Aaldea
Village(large)	Pueblo(m)	Pooeblo
Wall	Muro(m)	Mooro
Wall(city)	Muralla(f)	Muraalla
Watchmaker's shop	Relojería(f)	Relokhería
Youth hostel	Albergue juvenil	Albcrgay khuvenil

Do I need to book?
¿Tengo qur reservar?
¿Tengo ke reservar?

I would like to confirm my ticket.
Me gustaría confirmar mi billete.
Me goostaría konfirmar mi billete.

It's full.
Está completo.
Está kompleto.

I would like to change my ticket.
Me gustaría cambiar mi billete.
Me goostaría kambiar mi billete.

I would like to cancel my ticket.
Me gustaría cancelar mi billete.
Me goostaría kanthelar mi billete.

Two tickets for the. . .tomorrow,please.
Duas entradas al/a la. . .de la mañana,por favor.
Dooas entradas al/a la . . .de la maniana,por favor.

Are children allowed?
¿Se admiten niños?
¿Se admiten ninios?

Two child's ticket,please.
Dos billetse infantiles,por favor.
Dos billetes infantiles,por favor.

Is transport included?
¿Incluye transporte?
¿Inkluye transporte?

Do I need to take food with me?
¿Necesito llevar comida?
¿Nethesito llevar komida?

Is lunch included?
¿Se incluye el almuerzo?
¿Se inkluye l aalmooertho?

Everything included.
Todo incluido.
Todo inkluido.

I would like a guidebook in English.
Quisiera una guía turística en inglés.
Kisiera oona guía tooristika en inglés.

Do you have information on cultural sights?
¿Tiene información sobre los lugares de interés cultural?
¿Tiene information sobre los loogares de interés kultooral?

I want to see local sights.
Quiero ver los lugares de interés local.
Kiero ver los loogares de interés lokaal.

Can we hire a guide?
¿Podemos alquilar un guía?
¿Podemos alkilar oon guía?

I would like to see unique sights.
Me gustaría ver los lugares de interés único.
Me goostaría ver los loogare de interés ooniko.

Where do we meet?
¿Dónde nos reunimos?
¿Dónde nos reoonimos?

When do we meet?
¿A qué hora nos reunimos?
¿A ké ora nos reoonimos?

When do we start off?
¿Cuándo nos ponemos en camino?
¿Kuándo nos ponemos en kamino?

Will we be seeing the. . .too?
¿Visitaremos el/la . . .también?
¿Visitaremos l/la. .. también?

How much?
¿Cuánto?
¿Kuánto?

The guide will pay.
El guía va a pagar
L guía va a pagaar.

When do we get back?
¿A qué hora volvemos?
¿A ké ora volvemos?

Can you recommend somewhere cheap but nice.
¿Puede recomendar algún sitio barato pero agradable?
¿Pooede rekomendar algún sitio baraato pero agradaable?

Can you recommend somewhere luxurious?
¿Puede recomendar algún sitio de lujo?
¿Pooede rekomendar algún sitio lookho?

How long does the trip take?
¿Cuánto se tarda?
¿Kuánto se tarda?

When does . . .open?
¿Cuándo abre. . ?
¿Kuándo abre. . .?

When does . .close?
¿Cuándo cierra. . .?
¿Kuándo thierra. . .?

Will we have some free time?
¿Tendremos tiempo libre?
¿Tendremos tiempo libre?

Will be able to do some shopping?
¿Podremos hacer compras?
¿Podremos ather kompras?

Can you recommend somewhere romantic?
¿Puede recomendar algún sitio romántico?
¿Pooede rekomendar algún sitio romántiko?

What is the address?
¿Cuál es la dirección?
¿Kuál es la direkthión?

How long will we stay in. . .?
¿Hasta cuándo quedaremos en. . .?
¿Asta kuándo kedaremos en.. .?

Is it long route?
¿Es un viaje directo?
¿Es oon viakhe direkto?

What's worth seeing in. . .?
¿Qué vale visitar en. . .?
¿Ké vale visitar en . . ?

How much does the admission cost?
¿Cuánto cuesta la entrada?
¿Kuánta kuesta la entrada?

The guide has paid.
El guía ha pagado.
L guía a pagaado.

Is there an English speaking guide?
¿Hay un guía anglohablante?
¿Ay oon guía angloablaante?

I would like to see the. . .
Quisiera visitar el/la. . .
Kisiera visitar l /la. . .

Can we look at. . .today?
¿Podemos visitar . . .hoy?
¿Podemos visitar . . .oy?

When does the tour start?
¿Cuándo empieza el viaje?
¿Kuándo empietha l viakhe?

The tour includes two days at Andalusia.
El programa del viaje incluye una semana en Andalucía.
L programa del viakhe inkluye oona semaana en Andaluthía.

Can we take pictures?
¿Podemos sacar fotos?
¿Podemos sakar fotos?

What is this building/monument?
¿Qué es este edificio/monumento?
¿Qué es este edifithio/monumentò?

Who made it?
¿Quién lo hizo?
¿Kién lo hitho?

What time does it open/close?
¿A qué hora abren/cierran?
¿A ké ora abren/thierran?

What is the admission charge?
¿Cuánto cuesta la entrada?
¿Kuánto cuesta la entrada?

Is there a discount for groups?
¿Hay descuentos para grupos?
¿Ay deskuentos para groopos?

Who painted this picture?
¿Quién pintó esta pintura?
¿Kién pintó esta pintoora?

It is a painting of his early period.
Es un cuadro de su primera época.
Es oon kuadro de su primera épоka.

How old is it?
¿De qué época es?
¿De ké époka es?

It dates from 15th century
Data de siglo quince.
Data de siglo kinthe.

Could you take a photograoh of me here?
¿Me puede hacer una foto aquí?
¿Me pooede ather oona foto akí?

Why is the museum closed?
¿Por qué está cerrado el museo?
¿Por ké está therrado l mooseo?

Is it a national heritage?
¿Es un patrimonio nacional?
¿Es oon patrimonio nathional?

Where can I find?
¿Dónde puedo encontrar?
¿Dónde pooedo enkontrar?

Where are the toilets?
¿Dónde están los servicios?
¿Dónde están los servithios?

We are just touring around.
Hacemos visitas de turismo aquí y allí
Athemos visitas de toorismo akí y allí.

It is a monument to Columbus.
Es un monumento de Colón.
Es un monumento de Kolón.

I am lost.
Estoy perdido/a
Estoy perdido/a.

I have lost my group.
He perdido a mi grupo.
E perdido a mi groopo.

Where's the nearest beach?
¿Dónde está la playa más cercana?
¿Dónde está la playa más therkana?

Where's the nudist/best beach?
¿Dónde está la playa nudista/mejor?
¿Dónde está la playa noodista/mekhor?

Is it safe to dive/swim here?
¿Es seguro bucear/nadar aquí?
¿Es segooro buthear/nadar akí?

What time is high/low tide?
¿A qué hora es la marea alta/baja?
¿A ké ora es la marea aalta/bakha?

How much to rent a chair/an umbrella?
¿Cuánto por alquilar una silla/un parasol?
¿Kuánto por alkilar oona silla/oon parasol?

When is the next daytrip?
¿Cuándo es la próxima excursión de un día?
¿Kuándo es la próxima excursión de oon día?

Chapter 2

Directions
Direcciones

English	Spanish	Pronunciation
Behind	detrás de	detrás de
East	este(m)	este
Far away	lejos	lckhos
Here	aquí	akí
In front of	enfrente de	enfrente de
Left	por la izquierda	por la ithkierda
Near	cerca	therka
Next to	al lado de	aal lado de
North	norte(m)	norte
North-east	noreste(m)	noreste
North-west	noroeste(m)	noroeste
Opposite	frente a	frente a
Right	por la derecha	por la derecha
South	sur(m)	soor
South-east	sudeste(m)	soodeste
South-west	suroeste(m)	sooreste
Straight ahead	todo recto	todo rekto
There	ahí	aí
Turn	doble	doble
Turn left	doble a la izquierda	doble a la-ithkierda
Turn right	doble a la derecha	doble a la derecha
West	oeste(m)	oeste

To face in direction
Estar orientado en una dirección
Estar orientaado en oona direkthión

Face this way!
¡Vuélvase hacia aquí!
¡Vooélvase athia akí!

Turn at the corner.
Doble en la esquina.
Doble en le eskina.

Turn at the traffic lights.
Doble en el semáforo.
Doble en la semáforo.

Chapter 3

On The Plane
En El Avion

English	Spanish	Pronunciation
Aircraft	Avión(m)	Avión
Airport taxes	Impuestos(mpl) de-aeropuerto	Impooestos de-aeropooerto
Air sickness	Mareo(m)en avión	Mareo en avión
Arrival	Llegada(f)	Llegaada
Cancel	Suspender(v)	Soospender
Charter flight	Vuelo(m)chárter	Vooelo chárter
Charter plane	Avión(m)chárter	Avión charter
Check in	Facturar el equipaje	Fakturar l ekipakhe
Connecting flight	Vuelo(m)de enlace	Vooelo de enlathe
Crew	Tripulación(f)	Tripulathión
Custom clearance	Despacho(m)aduanal	Despacho adooanal
Custom declaration	Declaración(f)aduanera	Deklarathión-adooanera
Custom duty	Derechos(mpl)de aduana	Derechos adooana
Custom inspection	Revisión(f)aduanera	Revisión-adooanera
Custom service	Aduana(f)	Adooana
Delay	Retrasar(v)	Retrasar
Departure board	Tablón(m)de salidas	Tablón de salidas
Departure gate	Puerta(f)de embarque	Pooerta de-embarke
Departure lounge	Sala(f) de embarque	Sala de embarke
Departure time	Hora(f)de salida	Ora de salida

Destination	Destino(m)	Destino
Domestic flight	Vuelo(m)nacional	Vooelo nathionaal
Duty-free	Libre de impuestos	Libre de-impooestos
Economy class	Clase(f)económica	Klase ekonómika
Emergency exit	Salida(f)de urgencia	Saalida de-Oorkhenthia
Excess baggage	Exceso(m)de equipaje	Extheso de ekipakhe
Excess weight	Exceso(m)de peso	Exceso de peso
Fare	Precio(m)	Prethio
First class	Primera clase(f)	Primera klase
Flight	Vuelo(m)	Vooelo
Flight attendant	Auxiliar(m,f)de vuelo	Auxiliaar de vooelo
Flying time	Horas(fpl)de vuelo	Oras de vooelo
Fog	Niebla(f)	Niebla
Hand-luggage	Equipaje(m)de mano	Ekipakhe de maano
Helicopter	Helicóptero(m)	Elikóptero
Information	Información(f)	Informathión
Land	Aterrizar(v)	Aterrithar
Landing	Aterrizaje(m)	Aterrithakhe
Life-jacket	Chaleco(m) de-salvavidas	Chaleko de-salavidas
Luggage	Equipaje(m)	Ekipakhe
One way journey	Viaje(m)sin retorno	Viakhe sin retorno
One way ticket	Billete(m)sencillo	Billete senthillo
Passenger	Lista de pasakheros	Lista de-pasakheros
Passenger list	Lista(f)de pasajeros	Lista de-pasakheros
Pilot	Piloto(m,f)	Piloto

Plane	Avión(m)	Avión
Return flight	Vuelo(m)de regreso	Vooelo de regreso
Return journey	Viaje(m)de vuelta	Viaje(m) de vooelta
Return ticket	Billete de ida(f) y vuelta	Billete de ida y-Vooelta
Round trip	Ida(f) y vuelta	Ida y vooelta
Round trip ticket	Billete de ida(f)y vuelta	Billete de ida y-vooelta
Route	Ruta(f)	Roota
Scheduled flight	Vuelo(m) regular	Vooelo regoolaar
Scheduled stop	Parada(f)prevista	Paarada prevista
Seatbelt	Cinturón(m)de seguridad	Thinturón de-segooridad
Shuttle service	Puento(m)áereo	Pooento áereo
Take off	Despegue(m)	Despegay
Take off	Despegar(v)	Despegaar
Ticket	Billete(m)	Billete
Wating room	Sala(f) de espera	Sala de espera
Wing	Escuadrilla(f)	Eskuadrilla

We need three seats on an early flight to. . .
Necesitamos tres plazas en el primer vuelo en que las haya a . . .
Nethesitamos tres plathas en l primer vooelo en ke las aya. a . . .

When is the plane due?
¿Cuándo debe aterriazar el avión?
¿Kuándo debe aterrizar l avión?

What time do I check in?
¿A qué hora tengo que facturar mi equipaje?
¿A ké ora tengo ke fakturar mi ekipakhe?

Your papers please.
La documentación por favor
La dokumentathión por favor

Please give full particulars.
Se ruega dar un informe detallada.
Se rooega dar una informe detallada.

His papers are in order.
Tiene los papeles en regla.
Tiene los papeles en regla.

Is this passport in order?
¿Este pasaporte está en regla?
¿Este pasaporte está en regla?

I get sick in aeroplane.
Me mareo en el avión.
Me mareo en l avión.

Can I take this along as hand luggage?
¿Podría llevarlo como equipaje de mano?
¿Podría llevarlo komo ekipakhe de maano?

Does the plane make a stop at. . .?
¿Hace escala en. . .?
¿Athe eskala en. . .?

Has the plane from. . .already landed?
¿Ya ha aterrizado el avión de. . .?
¿Ya a aterrithado l avión de . . .?

How do I get to the airport?
¿Cómo puedo llegar al aeropuerto?
¿Kómo pooedo llegaar al aeropooerto?

How much is a (round-trip)flight to. . .?
¿Cuánto cuesta un vuelo (de ida y vuelta)a. . .?
¿Kuánto kooesta un vooelo(de ida y vooelta)a . . .?

I have to cancel my reservation.
Me veo obligado a cancelar la reservación.
Me veo obligaado a kanthelar la reservathión.

Is the plane to . . .late?
¿Está tarde el avión
¿Está tarde l avión?

How long will it be delayed?
¿Cuánto tiempo se retrasará?
¿Kuánto tiempo se retrasará?

Is there a connection to. . .?
¿Hay una correspondencia con. . .?
¿Ay una korrespondenthia kon. . .?

I would like to reserve a seat to . . .
Querría reservar una plaza a. . .
Kerría reservar una platha a. . .

What are they charging for luggage?
¿Cuánto piden por equipaje?
¿Kuánto piden por ekipakhe?

Where are we now?
¿Dónde estamos ahora?
¿Dónde estamos ahora?

That's my seat.
Ése es mi asiento.
Ése es mi asiento.

Where is the duty-free shop?
¿Dónde está la tienda libre de impuestos?
¿Dónde está la tienda libre de impooestos?

Where is the information office?
¿Dónde está el centro de informaciones?
¿Dónde está l thentro de informathiones?

When does the plane land?
¿Cuándo aterriza el avión?
¿Kuándo aterritha l avión?

Can you tell me when we get to...?
¿Me podría decir cuándo lleguemos a. . .?
¿Me podría dethir kuándo llegaymos a. . . ?

My luggage hasn't arrived.
Mis maletas se han perdido.
Mis maletas se an perdido.

My luggage has been damaged.
Mis maletas han sido dañadas.
Mis maletas an sido daniadas.

My luggage has been stolen.
Mis maletas se han robadas.
Mis maletas se an robaadas.

My luggage has been lost.
Mis maletas se han perdidas.
Mis maletas se an perdidas.

Chapter 4

Customs
Aduanas

Do you have anything to declare?
¿Tiene algo que declarar?
¿Tiene algo ke deklarar?

I have articles for my personal use.
Tengo artículos de uso personal.
Tengo artíkoolos de ooso personal.

That isn't mine.
Ese no es mío/mía.
Ese no es mío/mía.

Please open!
¡Por favor abra!
¡Por favor abra!

This is a present.
Este es un regla.
Este es un regla.

I have cigarillos.
Tengo cigarillos.
Tengo thigarillos.

That's my suitcase.
Esa maleta es mía.
Esa maleta es mía.

I would like to declare . . .
Querría declarar. . .
Querría deklarar. . .

Do i have to pay duty on. . .?
¿Tengo que pagar derechos de aduana por. . .?
¿Tengo ke pagar derechos de adooana por. . .?

It's a bottle of perfume.
Es un frasco de perfume.
Es un frasko de perfoome.

It belongs to me.
Es mío.
Es mío.

Chapter 5

At The Restaurant
En El Restaurante

Which local dishes do you recommend?
¿Cuáles platos típicos puedes recomendar?
¿Kuáles plaatos típikos pooedes rekomendar?

Is there a good Chinese restaurant here?
¿Hay un buen restaurante chino aquí.
¿Ay un buen restaoraante chino akí.

Which restaurant is the cheapest here?
¿Cuál restaurante es el más barato aquí?
¿Kuál restooraante es l más baraato akí?

Is there a vegetarian restaurant here?
¿Hay un restaurante vegetariano por aquí?
¿Ay oon restoorante vekhetariano akí?

I would like to reserve a table for three people.
Quisiera reservar una mesa para tres personas.
Kisiera reservar oona mesa para tres personas.

Are you still serving food?
¿Siguen sirviendo comida?
¿Sigayen sirviendo komida?

Where would you like to sit?
¿Dónde le gustaría sentarse?
¿Dónde la goostaría sentarse?

Is it self-service?
¿Es de autoservicio?
¿Es de aootoservithio?

Waiter!/Waitress
¡Camarero!Señorita!
¡Kamarero!Seniorita!

Have you ordered ?
¿Ha pedido ?
¿A pedido?

Would you like a drink while you wait?
¿Quiere tomar algo mientras espera?
¿Kiere tomar algo mientras espera?

What is the menu?
¿Cuál es el menu?
¿Kuál es l menu?

I would like to taste a local speciality.
Quisiera probar un plato típico.
Kisiera probar oon plato típiko.

Do you have a menu in English?
¿Tienen un menú en inglés?
¿Tienen oon menú en inglés?

Do you have children's meals?
¿Tienen comidas para niños?
¿Tienen komidas para ninios?

Is there a baby change room?
¿Hay una sala en la que cambiarle el pañal al bebé?
¿Ay oona sala en la ke kambiarle l panial al bebé?

Is there a highchair?
¿Hay una trona?
¿Ay oona trona?

Is there family discount?
¿Hay descuento familiar?
¿Ay deskuento faamiliaar?

Is there a child-minding service.
¿Hay servicio de cuidado de niños?
¿Ay servithio dc kuidado de ninios?

I would like to see the drink list.
Quisiera ver la lista de bebidas.
Kisiera ver la lista de bebidas.

Are these complimentary?
¿Éstos son gratis?
¿Éstos son gratis?

We only want drinks.
Sólo queremos tomar algo.
Sólo keremos tomar algo.

Please bring a glass.
Por favor nos trae un vaso.
Por favor nos trae oon vaso.

Please bring a serviette/a wineglass.
Por favor nos trae una servilleta/una copa de vino.
Por favor nos trae oona servilleta/oona kopa de vino.

How long is the wait?
¿Cuánto hay que esperar?
¿Kuánto ay ke esperar?

What shall we start off with?
¿Con qué empezamos?
¿Kon ké empethamos?

Is this seat taken?
¿Está ocupado este asiento?
¿Está okupaado este asiento?

Would you like a drink, sir?
¿Quisiera tomar algo,señor?
¿Kisiera tomar algo,senior?

Some water,please.
Agua,por favor.
Agooa,por favor.

Yes I would like to have. . .
Sí,quiero tomar . . .
Sí,kiero tomar. . .

I am on a . . .diet.
Sigo un régimen.
Sigo un rékhimen.

I don't eat red meat.
No como carne roja.
No komo karne rokha.

Could I have some of that chese.
¿Me puede servir un poco de ese queso?
¿Me puede servir un poko de ese keso?

Have another helping.
¿Otra ración?
¿Otra rathión?

I really couldn't.
No puedo.
No puedo.

It is fresh from the oven.
Está acabadito de salir del horno.
Está akabadito de saalir del orno.

Is it cooked with/in butter?
¿Esta cocinado con/en mantequilla?
¿Esta kothinado kon/en mantekilla?

I will check with the cook.
Le preguntaré al cocinero.
Le pregoontaré al kothinero.

What would you recommend?
¿Qué recomienda?
¿Ké rekomienda?

Could you prepare a meal without eggs/meat/fish?
¿Me puede preparar una comida sin huevo/carne/pescado?
¿Me pooede preparar oona komida sin ooevo/karne/peskado?

I don't want it deep-fried.
No lo quiero frito en aceite.
No lo kiero frito en atheite.

I would like it steamed.
Lo quiero al vapor.
Lo kiero al vapor.

I would like it with the dressing on the side.
Lo quiero con el aliño aparte.
Lo kiero kon l alinio apaarte.

Does it take long to prepare?
¿Tarda mucho en prepararse?
¿Tarda moocho en prepararse?

What is in that dish?
¿Que lleva ese plato?
¿Ke lleva ese plaato?

Is this free of animal produce?
Esto es sin productos de animales?
Esto es sin prodooktos de animaales?

A pot of coffee for two.
Café para dos.
Café para dos.

I like my meat well done.
Me gusta la carne muy hecha.
Me goosta la karne muy echa.

Help yourself!
¡Sírvete!/¡Sírvele!
¡Sírvete!/Sírvele!

They treated to him to a dinner.
Le obsequiaron con un banquete.
Le obsekiaron kon un bankete.

It's my treat.
Invito yo.
Invito yo.

Have you tried these. . .
¿Ha probado estas. . .?
¿A probaado estas. . .?

I love this dish.
Me encanta este plato.
Me enkanta esta plato.

This is burnt/too cold.
Esto está quemado/muy frío.
Esto está kemado/muy frío.

This is superb.
Esto está exquisito.
Esto está exkisito.

My bill,please.
La cuenta,por favor.
La kooenta,por favor.

Could we have separate bills.
Queremos cuentas individuales.
Keremos kuentaas individooales.

May I have a dance with you?
¿Quieres bailar?
¿Kieres bailaar?

Sorry i can't dance.
Lo siento,pero no puede.
Lo siento,pero no pooede.

Will you have some more?
¿Quieres más?
¿Kieres más?

Ice cream with a banana flavour.
Un helado con un sabor a plátano.
Un helado kon un sabor a plátano.

Should I add milk in you coffee?
¿Prefiere echar leche a su café?
¿Prefiere echar leche a su kafé?

I want to have a cigarette.May I?
Quiero fumar un pitillo.¿Me permite?
Kiero foomaar un pitillo.¿Me permite?

You may/may not smoke.
Se permite /prohíbe fumar.
Se permite/proíbe foomar.

Is service included in the bill?
¿Se incluye el servicio en la cuenta?
¿Se inkluye l servithio en la kuenta?

10% service is included.
Se incluye un 10 por ciento de servicio.
Se inkluye un 10 por thiento de servithio.

It's a especiality here.
Es un plato especial aquí.
Es un plaato espethial akí.

You have billed me for. . .euros instead of. . .
Usted ha puesto . . .euros y no . . .en la cuenta.
Usted a pooesto . . .euros y no. . .en la kooenta.

We love the local cuisine.
Nos encanta la comida típica de la zona.
Nos enkanta la komida típika de la thona.

That was delicious!
¡Estaba buenísimo!
¡Estaba buenísimo!

Chapter 6

At The Bar
En El Bar

A double whisky.
Un whisky doble.
Un whisky doble.

Cheers!
¡Salud!
¡Saalood!

Do you like soda with it?
¿Le echo un poco de sifón?
¿Le echo un poko de sifón?

Do you serve meals here?
¿Sirven comidas aquí?
¿Sirven komidas akí?

Excuse me!
¡Oiga!
¡Oiga!

Here's to you.
¡Vaya por ti!
¡Vaya por ti!

How much is that?
¿Cuánto es eso?
¿Kuánto es eso?

I am feeling drunk.
Esto me está subiendo mucho.
Esto me está soobiendo moocho.

I am next.
Ahora voy yo.
Aora voy yo.

I prefer gin and soda.
Prefiero ginebra con sifón.
Prefiro khinebra kon sifón.

I think I have had too many.
Creo que he tomado demasiado.
Kreo ke e tomado demasiado.

It's my round.
Es mi ronda.
Es mi ronda.

I will buy you a drink.
Te invito a una copa.
Te invito a oona kopa.

Let me treat you to a drink.
Permíteme invitarle a tomar algo.
Permíteme invitarle a tomar algo.

No ice, thanks.
Sin hielo, gracias.
Sin ielo, grathias.

Round of drinks, please.
Ronda de bebidas, por favor.
Ronda de bebidaas, por favor.

Same again, please.
Otra de lo mismo.
Otra de lo mismo.

Thanks,but I don't feel like it.
Lo siento, pero no me apetece.
Lo siento, pero no me apetethe.

The wine is extra.
El vino no está incluido.
L vino no está inkluido.

This drink is 40% proof.
Esta bebida tiene una graduación de 40 por 100.
Esta bebida tiene una graduathión de 40 por 100.

This is hitting the spot.
Me lo estoy pasando muy bien.
Me lo estoy pasando muy bien.

We drink it straight.
Lo bebemos sin mezcla.
Lo bebemos sin methkla.

Will you have a drink?
¿Quieres tomar algo?
¿Kieres tomar algo?

Whisky with a splash of water,please.
Whisky con un poquitín de agua,por favor.
Whisky kon un pokitín de agua,por favor

You can get the next one.
La próxima la pagas tú.
La próxima la pagas tú.

Chapter 7

At The Hotel
En El Hotel

-Do you have any accommodation available?
¿Tiene usted habitación disponible?
¿Tiene usted abitathión disponible?

I would like to book a room,please.
Quisiera reservar una habitación.
Kisiera oona reservar oona abitathión.

How much is it per night/week for a person?
¿Cuánto cuesta por noche/semana por una persona?
¿Kuánto kuesta por noche/semana por oona persona?

I already tried 2 hotels but they had no room.
Ya pregunté en 2 hoteles pero no tenían habitación.
Ya pregoonté en 2 oteles pero no tenían abitathión.

I have a reservation.
He hecho una reservación.
E hecho oona reservathión.

Sorry we are full up for/till
Siento,no tenemos nada libre para/hasta
Siento,no tenemos nada libre para/asta

The hotel is booked up.
Todas las habitaciones del hotel están reservadas.
Todas las abitathiones del otel están reservadas.

Please book us in for Sunday.
Le ruego reservamos una habitación para el domingo.
Le rooego reservamos una abitathión para l domingo.

For two nights.
Por dos días.
Por dos días.

Single room or double?
¿Habitación individual o doble?
¿Abitathión individooaal o doble?

A.c. or non a.c.?
¿Climatizado o no climatizado?
¿Klimatithado o no klimatithado?

I would prefer a single/double a.c/non a.c room.
Prefería una habitación individual/doble climatizado/no climatizado.
Prefería una abitathión individooaal/doble klimatithado/no klimatithado.

For how many nights?
¿Por cuántas noches?
¿Por kuántas noches?

Yes,please check in here.
Sí,por favor firme el registro.
Sí,por favor firme l rekhistro.

I would prefer the top/ground/first floor,please.
Prefería el piso alto/bajo/primer,por favor
Prefería l piso aalto/bakho/primer,por favor.

What is the check out time?
¿Qué es la hora de salida?
¿Ké es la ora de salida?

How much extra to stay until 9o'clock?
¿Cuánto más cuesta quedarse hasta las nueve?
¿Kuánto más kuesta kedarse asta las nooeve?

Can I check out late?
¿Puedo dejar la habitación más tarde?
¿Pooedo dekhar la abitathión más tarde?

Can I see it?
¿Puedo verla?
¿Pooedo verla?

It's fine.i'll take it.
Vale,la alquilo.
Vale,la alkilo.

Can I pay by credit card/travellers cheque?
¿Puedo pagar con tarjeta de crédito/cheques de viajero?
¿Pooedo pagar kon tarkheta de krédito/cheke de viakhero?

Which is the room assigned to me?
¿Qué habitación es la que me destinan a mí?
¿Ké abitathión es la ke me destinaan a mí?

Is there a safe in this hotel?
¿Hay una caja fuerte en este hotel?
¿Ay oona kakha fooerte en este otel?

It's a service that has to be paid for.
Es un servicio que hay que pagar.
Es un servithio ke ay ke pagar.

You have to add . . .euros on for the service.
Hay que poner . . .euros más de servicio.
Ay ke poner. . .euros más de servithio.

'With the compliments of the management '
'Obsequio de la casa'
'Obsckio dc la kasa'

Is there a room reserved for wife and self?
¿Hay una habitación reservada para mi esposa y yo?
¿Ay una abıtathión reservada para mi esposa y yo?

Sorry but the service is poor in this hotel.
Siento pero en este hotel el servicio es malo.
Siento pero en este otel l servithio es maalo.

Is service included in the bill?
¿Se incluye el servicio en la cuenta?
¿Se inkluye l servithio en la kuenta

Yes,10% service is included.
Sí,se incluye un 10 por ciento de servicio.
Sí,se inkluye un10 por thiento de servithio.

Can I leave my bags here?
¿Puedo dejar las maletas aquí?
¿Pooedo dekhar las maletas akí?

Is there a swimming pool?
¿Hay piscina?
¿Ay pisthina?

Who is it?
¿Quién es?
¿Kién es?

Room service.please.
Servicio de habitación,por favor
Servithio de abitathión,por favor.

Just a moment.
Un momento.
Oon momento.

Come in!
¡Adelante!
¡Adelaante!

I am at your service.
Estoy a su disposición.
Estoy a su dispositión.

Could you come back later,please.
¿Puede volver más tarde,por favor?
¿Pooede volver más tarde,por favor?

You rang,sir/madam?
¿Me llama usted,señor/señora?
¿Me llama usted,senior/seniora?

Please wake me at cinco.
Por favor,despiérteme a las cinco.
Por favor,despiérteme a las thinko.

Is there any message for me?
¿Tiene un mensaje para mí?
¿Tiene oon mensakhe para mí?

Is there any post/parcel for me?
¿Hay cartas/paquete para mí?
¿Ay kartas/pakete para mí?

There is a parcel/letter for you.
Hay un paquete/carta para usted.
Ay un paakete/karta para usted.

From where did it come?
¿De dónde vino?
¿De dónde vino?

It came with the post.
Vino con el correo.
Vino kon l korreo.

When did it come?
¿Cuándo vino?
¿Kuándo vino?

It came this morning.
Vino esta mañana.
Vino esta maniana.

There is a parcel/letter addressed to Mr.Fernando.
Hay un pakete/carta con el nombre de Señor Fernando.
Ay un paakete/karta kon l nombre de Senior Fernando.

When/Where's breakfast served?
¿Cuándo/Dónde se sirve el desayuno?
¿Kuándo/Dónde se sirve l desayoono?

Can I use the laundry?
¿Puedo usar el lavadero?
¿Pooedo oosar l lavadero?

Do you also arrange tours?
¿También organizan recorridos?
¿Tambien organithan rekorridos?

Can you call a taxi for me?
¿Me puede pedir un taxi?
¿Me pooede pedir oon taxi?

Can I use your telephone?
¿Podría usar su teléfono?
¿Podría oosar su teléfono?

I am leaving now.
Me voy ahora.
Me voy aora.

Could I have my deposit please?
¿Me puede dar mi depósito?
¿Me pooede dar mi depósito?

Could I have my valuables back?
¿Me puede devolver mis objetos de valor?
¿Me pooede devolver mis obkhetos de valor?

Did you have a pleasant stay?
¿Ha tenido una estancia muy agradable?
¿A tenido oona estanthia muy agradable?

Yes!
¡Sí!

Chapter 8

Complaints
Quejas

The shower/light does not work.
No funciona la ducha/lámpara.
No foonthiona la doocha/lámpara.

We will see to it.
Lo arreglaremos.
Lo arreeglaaremos.

The door of my room no.202 doesn't close properly.
La puerta de la habitación núm.202 cierra mal.
La pooerta de la abitathión núm.202 thierra maal.

Please have it repaired.
Por favor mándelo componer.
Por favor mándelo komponer.

The window does not open/close.
No se abre/cierra la ventana.
No se abre/thierra la ventana.

The lift is stuck at the seventh floor.
El ascensor se ha atrancado en el piso séptimo.
L asthensor se a atrankado en l piso séptimo.

I am locked out of my room.
Cerré la puerta y se me olvidaron las llaves dentro.
Therré la pooerta y se olvidaron las llaves dentro.

The air-conditioning/fan doesn't work.
No funciona el aire acondicionado/el ventilador.
No foonthiona l aire akondithionado/l ventilador.

The toilet is not clean.
El retrete no está limpio.
El retrete no está limpio.

There is a cockroach in the bathroom.
Hay una cucaracha en el baño.
Ay oona kukaracha en l banio.

The bathroom is locked.
La puerta de baño está cerrada.
La pooerta de banio está therrada.

The room is too dark.
El cuarto es demasiado oscuro.
L kuarto es demasiado oskuro.

The sheets are not clean.
Las sábanas no están limpias.
Las sábanaas no están limpias.

The room is too cold/small.
El cuarto es demasiado frío/pequeño.
L kuarto es demasiado frío/pekenio.

Chapter 9

On The Telephone
Al Telefono

Hello(making a call)
Hola.
Ola

Hello(answering a call)
¿Diga?
¿Diga?

Is Mr.García there?
¿Está Señor García?
¿Está Senior García?

Can I speak to. ..?
¿Está. . .?
¿Está. . .?

Speaking!
¡Al aparato!
¡Al apaaraato!

Yes,I am Carmen.Tell me.
Sí,soy Carmen.Dígame.
Sí,soy Karmen.Dígame.

Who is calling,please?
¿Me puede decir quién llama?
¿Me puede dethir kién llama?

Who do you want to speak to?
¿Con quién quiere hablar?
¿Kon kién kiere ablaar?

Where are you calling from?
¿Desde dónde llama usted?
¿Desde dónde llama usted?

I am calling from Madrid.
Llamo desde Madrid.
Llamo desde Madrid.

You have the wrong number.
Usted se ha equivocado de número.
Usted se a ekivokado de número.

What is your phone number?
¿Cuál es tu número de teléfono?
¿Kuál es tu noomero de teléfono?

Could you put me through to Mr.Lopéz?
¿Me pone con el Señor Lopéz?
¿Me pone kon l Senior Lopéz?

Whose call is it?
¿A quién le toca?
¿A kién le toka?

What number do you want?
¿Con qué número desea comunicar?
¿Kon ké número desea komunikar?

Can I take a message for him?
¿Quiere que le pase un recado?
¿Kiere ke le pase un rekado?

Please tell him I had called.
Por favor dile que he llamado.
Por favor dile ke e llamado.

Could you give me the number of. . .?
¿Me puede decir el número de. . .?
¿Me puede dethir l número de. . .?

Please speak after the tone.
Deje su mensaje después de la señal.
Dekhe su mensakhe despooés de la senial.

What is the code for India?
¿Cuál es el prefijo de la India.
¿Kuál es l prefikho de la India?

You omit the '0' when dialling England from Spain
No marque el 'cero' del prefijo cuando llame a Londres desde España.
No marke l 'thero' del prefikho kuando llame a Londres desde Espania.

Would you repeat the number please?
¿Podría repetir el número,por favor?
¿Podría repetir l número por favor?

Would you like to leave a message for him?
¿Quiere dejar un recado?
¿Kiere dekhar un rekado?

Can I dial direct to Delhi?
¿Puedo llamar a Delhi marcando directamente?
¿Puedo llamar a Delhi markando direktamente?

You can dial the number direct.
Puede marcar el número directamente.
Puede markar l número direktamente.

I want to make an international call.
Deseo llamar al extranjero.
Deseo llamae al extrankhero.

Would you give me an alarm call for 6.30 tomorrow morning please?
Por favor, ¿me podrían avisar por teléfono mañana por la mañana a las seis y media?
Por favor,¿me podrían avisar por teléfono maniana por la maniana a las seis y media?

There is no reply from. . .
El . . .no contesta.
L . . .no kontesta.

Please hold the line.
Por favor no se retire.
Por favor no se retire.

All lines are engaged,please try later.
Las líneas están saturadas,llame más tarde,por favor.
Las líneas están satooradas,llame más tarde,por favor

The line is busy.
Está comunicando.
Está komunikando.

I cannot get through.
No consigo comunicar.
No konsigo komunikar.

We have got a bad connection.
No se oye bien la línea.
No se oye bien la línea.

Please replace the receiver.
Cuelgue,por favor.
Kooelgay,por favor

The phone is out of order.
El teléfono está estropeado.
L teléfono está estropeado.

Where is the nearest public phone?
¿Dónde hay una cabina telefónica?
Dónde ay oona kabina telefónika?

How much does a one minute call cost?
¿Cuánto cuesta una llamada de un minuto?
¿Kuánto kuesta oona llamada de oon minuto?

I need an adaptor plug.
Necesito un adaptador.
Nethesito oon adaptador.

I have lost the charger for my phone.
He perdido el cargador de mi teléfono.
E perdido l kargador de mi teléfono.

I want a mobile/cell phone for hire for a week.
Quiero un móvil para alquilar por una semana.
Kiero oon móvil para alkilar por oona semana.

Do you have prepaid phone?
¿Hay una tarjeta prepagada?
¿Ay oona tarkheta prepagaada?

This is not the SIM card for your network.
Eso no es la tarkheta SIM para su red.
Eso no es la tarkheta SIM para su red.

Chapter 10

Asking The Way
Preguntar La Via

Am I right for the airport?
¿Por aquí se va al aeropuerto?
¿Por akí se va al aeropooerto.

Are we on the right way?
¿Vamos por buen camino?
¿Vamos por buen kamino?

'Can I give you a lift to the airport?
¿Quiere que le lleve al aeropuerto?
¿Kiere ke le lleve al aeropooerto?

Can you direct me to the market?
¿Podría indicarme la dirección del mercado?
¿Podría indikarme la direkthión del merkaado?

How can we go to the shortest way to the monument?
¿Cómo podemos tomar el camino más corto al monumento?
¿Kómo podemos tomaar l kamino más korto al monumento?

How far is it to the airport?
¿Cuánto hay de aquí al aeropuerto?
¿Kuánto ay de akí al aeropooerto?

It's a long drive.
Es un trayecto largo.
Es un trayekto largo.

It's a short car run.
Es un breve viaje en coche.
Es un breve viakhe en koche.

It's two blocks away.
Eso queda a dos calles.
Eso keda dos kalles.

Is this the right place?
¿Es este el lugar correcto?
¿Es este l loogaar korrekto?

Is this the road for. . .?
¿Es éste el camino de. . .?
¿Es éste l kamino de. . .?

Is it far?
¿Está lejos?
¿Está lekhos?

It is on the other side of the street.
Está al otro lado de la calle.
Está al otro laado de la kalle

It is in the direction of . . .
Está por el lado de. . .
Está por l laado de. . .

It is 10 kilometres to the palace.
De aquí al palacio hay 10 kilómetros.
De akí al paalathio ay 10 kilómetros.

This isn't the way to. ..
Por aquí no se va. . .
Por akí no se va. . .

This road leads back to the hotel.
Por este camino se vuele al hotel.
Por ese kamino vooele al otel.

This road meets up with the motorway.
Esta carretera empalma con la autopista.
Esta karretera empalma kon la aootopista.

This street leads to. . .
Esta calle conduce a. . .
Esta kale konduthe a . . .

Take the first on the right.
Vaya por la primera calle a la derecha.
Vaya por la primera kalle a la derecha.

We take the road to. ..
Vamos por el camino de. . .
Vamos por l kamino de. . .

We have a long way to go
Tenemos mucho camino por delante.
Tenemos mucho kamino por delaante.

We took the wrong road.
Nos equivocamos de camino.
Nos ekivokamos de kamino.

Where are you bound for?
¿Adónde se dirige usted?
¿Adónde se dirikhe usted?

Where do we go from here?
¿Adónde vamos desde aquí?
¿Adónde vamos desde akí?

Where does this road lead?
¿Adónde conduce este camino?
¿Adónde konduthe este kamino?
Can you show me on the map?
¿Me lo puede indicar en la mapa?
¿Me pooede indikar en la mapa?

Which is the way to the station,please.
Por favor,¿qué camino tomo para ir a la estación?
Por favor,¿ké kaamino tomo parair a la estathión?

Which way to the airport?
¿Por dónde se va al aeropuerto?
¿Por dónde se va al aeropooerto?

You are a long way out.
Usted se ha extraviado bastante.
Usted se a extraviado bastaante.

Chapter 11

Taxi
Taxi

Is this taxi free?
¿Está libre este taxi?
¿Está libre este taxi?

Please put the meter on.
Por favor ponga el taxímetro.
Por favor ponga l taxímetro.

How much is it to. . .?
¿Cuánto cuesta ir a . . .?
¿Kuánto kuesta ir a . . .?

Please take me to this address.
Por favor lléveme a esta dirección.
Por favor lléveme a esta direkthión.

How much is the final fare?
¿Cuánto es en total?
¿Kuánto es l totaal?

Please slow down.
Por favor vaya más despacio.
Por favor vaya más despathio.

Please wait here.
Por favor espere aquí.
Por favor espere akí.

Stop at the corner!
¡Pare en la esquina!
¡Pare en la eskina!

Stop here!
¡Pare aquí!
¡Pare akí!

Chapter 12

In The Police Station
En La Comisaria

I would like to report a theft.
Quisiera hacer una denuncia de robo.
Kisiera ather oona denoonthia de robo.

I have lost my passport/purse.
He perdido mi pasaporte/bolsa.
E perdido mi pasaporte/bolsa.

I have been robed.
Me han robado.
Me aan robado.

I am not guilty.
Soy inocente.
Soy inothente.

I want to contact my embassy/consulate.
Quiero ponerme en contacto con mi embajada/consulado.
Kiero ponerme en kontakto kon mi embakhada/konsoolado.

Can I call a lawyer?
¿Puedo llamar a un abogado?
¿Pooedo llamar a oon abogado?

I need a lawyer who speaks English.
Necesito un abogado que hable inglés.
Nethesito oon abogado ke able inglés.

It's not my fault.
Yo no tengo la culpa.
Yo no tengo la koolpa.

I apologise.
Lo siento.
Lo siento.

Can I pay an on-the-spot fine?
¿Puedo pagar una multa al contado?
¿Pooedo pagar oona moolta al kontado?

Chapter 13

In The Bank
En El Banco

Where can I . . .?
¿Dónde puedo. . .?
¿Dónde pooedo?

I would like to cash a cheque.
Me gustaría cambiar un cheque.
Me goostaría kambiar oon cheke.

I would like to change money.
Me gustaría cambiar dinero.
Me goostaría kambiar dinero.

What time does the bank open?
¿A que hora abre el banco?
¿A ke ora abre l banko?

Can I arrange a transfer?
¿Puedo hacer una transferencia?
¿Pooedo ather oona transferenthia?

I have forgotten my PIN no.
Me he olvidado del número de NPI.
Me e olvidaado del noomero de NPI

What is the exchange rate?
¿Cuál es el tipo de cambio?
¿Kuál es l tipo de kambio?

Can I see your passport,please?
¿Puedo ver su pasaporte,por favor?
¿Pooedo ver su pasaporte,por favor?

Chapter 14

In The Post Office
En Correos

Where is the post office?
¿Dónde está la oficina de correos?
¿Dónde está la ofithina de korreos?

Where is the post office box/mail box?
¿Dónde está el apartado de correos/el buzón?
¿Dónde está l aparataado de koreros/l buthón?

I want to send a fax/parcel.
Quisiera enviar un fax/un paquete.
Kisiera enviar oon fax/oon pakete.

I want to buy an aerogram/envelope.
Quisiera comprar un aerograma/un sobre.
Kisiera komprar oon aerograama/oon sobre.

Is there any post for me?
¿Hay cartas para mí?
¿Ay kartas para mí?

What is the postage on this letter?
¿Cuánto franqueo lleva esta carta?
¿Kuánto frankeo lleva esta karta?

Chapter 15

At The Border
En La Frontera

Your passport/visa please.
Su pasaporte/visado,por favor.
Su pasaporte/visado,por favor.

Are you travelling in a group/with family?
¿Está viajando en un grupo/con una familia?
¿Está viakhando en oon grupo/kon oona familia?

Are you travelling on your own?
¿Está viajando solo?
¿Está viakhando solo?

Your papers,please.
La documentación,por favor.
La dokumentathión,por favor.

What is your purpose of visit?
¿Qué es el motivo del viaje?
¿Ké es l motivo del viakhe?

I am on business here.
Estoy aquí de negocios.
Estoy akí de negothios.

I am here on holiday.
Estoy aquí de vacaciones.
Estoy akí de vakathiones.

I am here for 2 days/1 month.
Estoy aquí por 2 días/1 mes.
Estoy aquí por 2 días/1 mes.

I am here for 2 weeks.
Estoy aquí por 2 semanas.
Estoy akí por 2 semanas.

I have nothing to declare.
No tengo nada que declarar.
No tengo nada ke deklarar.

Chapter 16

Socialising
Salir

Are you free tomorrow?
Estás libre manaña?
Estás libre maniana.

What are you doing this evening?
¿Qué haces esta noche?
¿Ké athes esta noche?

What are doing now?
¿Qué haces ahora?
¿Ké athes aora?

Would you like to go for a meal/drink?
¿Quieres que vayamos a comer/tomar algo?
¿Kieres ke vayamos a komer/tomar algo?

Can you come to dinner?
¿Puedes venir a cenar?
¿Pooedes venir a thenar?

I will pick you up.
Paso a recogerte.
Paso a rekokherte.

Are you ready?
¿Estás listo/a?
¿Estás listo/a?

Yes, I am ready.
Sí, estoy listo/a.
Sí, estoy listo/a.

Let me treat you to a drink.
Permíteme invitarte a tomar algo.
Permíteme invitate a tomaar aalgo.

Will you join me in a drink?
¿Quieres tomar algo conmigo?
¿Kieres tomaar aalgo konmigo?

Would you like to go for a walk?
¿Quieres que vayamos a pasear?
¿Kieres ke vayamos a pasear?

May I join you?
¿Se permite?
¿Se permite?

Ok!
¡Hecho!
¡Echo!

I feel like going out somewhere.
Me apetece ir a salir.
Me apetethe ir a saalir

Chapter 17

At The Bookshop
En La Libreria

An english newspaper, please.
Un periódico inglés,por favor.
Oon periódiko inglés,por favor.

I need a map of the area.
Necesito un mapa de esta región.
Nethesito oon mapa de esta rekhión.

Today's paper,please.
El diario,por favor.
L diario,por favor.

I am looking for a jokebook in english.
Busco por un libro de chistes en inglés.
Busko por oon libro de chistes en inglés.

Chapter 18

Small Talk
Charla

Goodmorning,sir/madam!
¡Buenos días,señor/señora!
¡Buenos días,senior/seniora!

How are you?
¿Cómo está?
¿Kómo está?

Very well.
Muy bien.
Muy bien.

What is your name?
¿Cómo se llama?
¿Kómo se llama?

My name is. . .
Me llamo. . .
Me llamo. . .

Where do you come from?
¿De dónde es?
¿De dónde es?

I am from India.
Soy de India.
Soy de India.

Do you live here?
¿Vives aquí?
¿Vives akí?

Where are you going?
¿Adónde vas?
¿Adónde vas?

What are you doing?
¿Qué haces?
¿Ké athes?

What business are you in?
¿A qué se dedica usted?
¿A ké se dedika oosted?

Do you speak English?
¿Habla inglés?
¿Abla inglés?

I don't understand Spanish.
No comprendo el español.
No komprendo l espaniol.

Could you please speak more slowly?
¿Puedes por favor hablar más despacio?
¿Pooedes por favor ablar más despathio?

I can't speak Spanish.
No puedo hablar en español.
No pooedo ablar en espaniol.

I speak a little Spanish.
Hablo un poco de español.
Ablo oon poko de espaniol.

Are you married?
¿Está casado/a?
¿Está kasado/a?

Yes,I am married./No I am not married.
Sí,estoy casado/a./No estoy casado/a.
Sí,estoy kasado/a./No estoy kasado/a.

When is your birthday?
¿Cuándo es tu cumpleaños?
¿Kuándo es tu koompleanios?

What is your age?
¿Cuántos años tiene?
¿Kuántos anios tiene?

I am 25 years old.
Tengo 25 años.
Tengo 25 anios.

What do you do?
¿Qué hace?
¿Ké áthe?

I am a writer.
Soy escritor/a.
Soy eskritor/a.

Have you come for the first time here?
¿Viene por la primera vez?
¿Viene por la primera veth?

How long do you plan to stay?
¿Cuánto tiempo piensa quedarte?
¿Kuánto tiempo piensa kedarte?

Another week/two weeks.
Otra semana/otras duas semanas.
Otra semana/otras dooas semanas.

It is very nice here.
Aquí se está muy bien.
Akí se está muy bien.

It's been great meeting you.
Me ha encantado conocerte.
Me a enkantado konotherte.

Keep in touch.
¡Nos mantendremos en contacto!
¡Nos mantendremos en kontakto!

With great pleasure.
Con mucho gusto.
Kon mucho gusto.

Whatever you like
Lo que quieras
Lo ke kieras

Ok(all right)
Está bien.
Está bien.

I am ok,thanks.
Estoy bien,gracias.
Estoy bien,grathias.

It's nice of you to help.
Usted es muy amable ayudándome.
Usted es muy amable ayudándome.

Were you waiting for me?
¿Me estaba esperando?
¿Me estaba esperando?

I don't like that.
No me gusta esto.
No me goosta esto.

No thanks.
No gracias.
No grathias

I have no fixed plans.
No he arreglado nada en definitivo.
No e arreglaado nada en definitivo.

Wait a moment!
¡Un momento!
¡Oon momento!

It does not matter.
No importa.
No importa.

Tomorrow is my last day here.
Mañana es mi último día aquí.
Maniana es mi ooltimo día akí.

I am here with my family.
Estoy aquí con mi familia.
Estoy akí kon mi familia.

I would like to introduce you to.
Quisiera presentarle a . . .
Quisiera presentarle a. . .

This is my child/colleague.
Éste/a es mi hijo/a.
Éste/a es mi ikho/a.

This is my friend.
Éste/a es mi amigo/a.
Éste/a es mi aamigo/a.

This is my wife/husband.
Éste/a es mi esposa/marido.
Éste/a es mi esposa/maarido.

Chapter 19

Greetings
Saludos

All the best!
¡Que tengas suerte!
¡Ke tengas suerte!

And the same to you!
¡Igualmente!
¡Igualmente!

Best wishes!
¡Felicidades!
¡Felithidades!

Certainly!
¡Por supuesto!
¡Por supuesto!

Certainly not!
¡De ninguna manera!
¡De ningoona maanera!

Congratulations!
¡Mis felicidades!
¡Mis felithidades!

Excuse me! (passing somebody)
¡Perdón!
¡Perdón!

Excuse me! (interrupting somebody)
¡Perdone usted!
¡Perdone usted!

Excuse me! (leaving table)
Con permiso
Kon permiso

Farewell
Despedida
Despedida

Fine
¡Estupendo!
¡Estupendo!

Christmas greetings
Felicitación de la Navidad
Felithitathión de la Navidad

Good!
¡Bueno!
¡Bueno!

Goodmorning
Buenos días
Buenos días

Goodafternoon
Buenas tardes
Buenas tardes

Goodevening
Buenas tardes
Buenas tardes

Goodnight
Buenas noches
Buenas noches

Goodbye
¡Adiós!
¡Adios

Happy new year
¡Feliz año nuevo!
¡Felith anio nooevo!

Have a good trip!
¡Tengas buen viaje!
¡Tengas buen viakhe!

Hope you have a lovely time!
¡Que os divirtáis!
¡Ke os divirtáis!

How are you?
¿Cómo está?
¿Kómo está?

I am fine
Estoy bien
Estoy bien

I am pleased to meet you
Tengo mucho gusto en conocerle
Tengo mucho gusto en konotherle

I see!
¡Ya!
¡Ya!

I went to give him my best wishes
Fui a darle la enhorabuena
Fui a darle la enorabuena

Mention not
De nada
De nada

Merry Christmas
¡Felices Pascuas!
¡Felithes Paskuas

Okay
¡Vale!, ¡bien!
¡Vale!,¡bien!

Please God
Plegue a Dios
Plegay a Dios